The Chemistry of Growth

The Chemistry of Growth

A CEO's Guide

JOHN W. MYRNA

Copyright © 2023 by John W. Myrna

All rights reserved.

No part of this book may be reproduced or used in any manner without the prior written permission of the copyright owner, except for the use of brief quotations in a book review.

To request permissions, contact John W. Myrna at tcog@myrna.com.

Published by QuickStudy Press
ISBN: 979-8-9879795-0-1

The Expansion Matrix™, The Platinum Paradigm™, The Progress Accelerator™, and The Progress Pyramid™ are trademarks of Myrna Associates, Inc.

Contents

Foreword   vii

The Pledge   ix

Introduction: In Search of the Philosopher's Stone   1

Chapter 1: The Chemistry of Growth   7

Chapter 2: The Chemistry of an Executive Leadership Team   15

Chapter 3: Team Planning: The Catalyst for Successful Strategy   33

Chapter 4: The Good, the Bad, and the Ugly Truth About Growth   53

Chapter 5: Market, Technical, and Financial Risk   67

Chapter 6: The Chemistry of Product/Market Strategies   83

Chapter 7: Organizing to Win   99

Chapter 8: Productivity and Continuous Improvement   113

Chapter 9: The Chemistry of Implementation   125

Chapter 10: People Chemistry: Engaged, Empowered, and Accountable   149

Conclusion: The Chemistry of Breakthrough Leadership   167

Definitions	173
Resources	177
Acknowledgements	179
About the Author	181
Index	183

Dedication

This book is dedicated to Mary, my partner in business and life. I would have been truly a lost soul without her insight and gentle coaching over the years.

Foreword

"Destiny is no matter of chance. It is a matter of choice. It is not a thing to be waited for, it is a thing to be achieved."

William Jennings Bryan

"Everything should be made as simple as possible, but not simpler."

Albert Einstein

Defining moments. We all have them. Those times in our careers where one decision among many changes the course and landscape of our future. In reflecting on the success my partner and I achieved with our business, it was clear to us that meeting, and then engaging, John Myrna was one of those defining moments.

Over a ten-year period, we learned and applied the strategic planning tools John developed. These tools enabled us to become a professionally managed, fiscally sound organization; they contributed to a five-fold increase in earnings and helped us create one of the most highly regarded firms in our market space.

We had always understood the importance of strategic planning, but found the traditional approaches lacking in the two most essential criteria of all – year in and year out engagement and results. Many of you may have the same mental picture of strategic planning as we did – a one- or two-week off-site meeting with lots of conversation and feeling distracted by thoughts of the "real" work back at the office. And of course, the three-ring summary binder that ultimately never found its way off the shelf after that meeting.

We knew there had to be a better way, and in that defining moment, we found it. John's two-day approach resonated with what we felt we needed – a simpler approach, one that did not require an extended time frame and one that we could use in real time to bring our vision of the future to life.

We reframed strategy as a direction, not a goal. We felt that strategy had to be believable and executable, so we created guardrails, the four to six activities that we needed to be preoccupied with every day. These helped to keep us on track and to remind us what actions were or were not permitted to ensure we stayed focused on the tasks aimed at producing results.

And perhaps most importantly, we learned how to work as a team, which, at the end of the day, is what success is all about.

You may be asking, why another book on strategic planning? After all, a search of Amazon produces over 60,000 results. I think the answer is straightforward. Over the last few years, I had suggested to John that it would be a good idea if he would consider taking his lifetime of ideas, principles, tools and successes, and organize them into a book. Such a book would create a short course on how to bring visions of success to life and help companies replace the dusty binder on the shelf with bottom-line results.

Good ideas are ideas that work. John's book is a good idea. It works. Anyone interested in improving the odds of achieving their goals, of bringing their vision of the future to life, owes it to themselves to read John's book. And, to maybe even spend two days with John. After all, what have you got to lose…other than your dreams?

Robert Posten
Chairman, Comanche Holdings, LLC
and former co-president, TNS Landis

The Pledge

Put your hand over your heart and repeat after me:

"I will never do something stupid."

Go ahead, trust me.

"I will never do something stupid because of something written on a sheet of paper."

This book, and the strategic plans you develop based on its concepts, are tools to enhance focus and communications. They are not a license to do stupid things.

This is a pledge that I have every member of every planning team take when we are working to define their strategy. Strategy is the collective set of answers to the questions about *what* we want the future to look like, *why*, and *how* to make it happen. Effective strategy requires specifics, such as these examples:

- Grow revenue to $25 million within five years.
- Identify and grow a new market to account for at least 10 percent of revenue.

- Reduce dependence on our largest customer to under 25 percent.

Executives are typically unwilling to volunteer specific numbers, based on concerns that doing so will contribute to their team making stupid decisions in the future, such as:

- Allowing managers to use planning numbers as clubs to beat them with,
- Not adjusting to new information and changes in the environment, or
- Missing serendipitous opportunities.

This pledge, and utilizing the processes of strategic planning that incorporate ongoing adjustment, frees you to develop, implement, and manage the right strategies for your company's success.

Introduction

In Search of the Philosopher's Stone

"Where you are headed is more important than how fast you are going. Rather than always focusing on what's urgent, learn to focus on what is really important."

Anonymous

"I am tomorrow, or some future day, what I establish today. I am today what I established yesterday or some previous day."

James Joyce

My introduction to strategy and expectancy management

At the first executive strategy session I ever participated in, way back in 1976, I experienced an epiphany. As a passionate, intelligent engineering executive, albeit an inexperienced and newly minted one, I had been searching for the magic formula for business success. I pored over every business book, seeking the equivalent of the philosopher's stone that would covert the company's leaden daily issues into precious gold. During that fateful planning meeting, I realized the stark differences between a company's yearly operating plan and a true strategic plan. My eyes lit up at the concept of "expectancy management," the practice of making decisions today based on where we wanted to be in the future.

Finally, my company had a better approach than mixing random strategic elements in the hope they would produce some sort of positive chemical reaction. (Random actions in the past had included hiring a PhD to do R&D without any staff or support, investing days in the hopeless pursuit of a multi-million-dollar government contract, and trying to sell excess capacity as a commodity.) Instead, now the company could visualize a desired future and combine the elements "scientifically" to create it.

A paradigm shift

Here was the answer – it wasn't one single, magical thing, it was a whole different paradigm. Before the meeting, my company had a corporate strategy best described as "just work harder." We had gone deeply into debt with a New England bank to double our capacity, not noticing the onset of a recession that had temporarily flattened our growth. In fact, it was pressure from the bank, worried at our worsening financials, that had pushed us into "wasting" our time planning strategy rather than fighting fires.

A short three years after that first executive strategy meeting, the company was able to execute a highly successful initial public offering, showcasing a string of profitable years unprecedented in our corporate history.

The chemistry of growth

With my engineer's perspective, I clearly saw there was an underlying chemistry that could be used to dramatically transform today's tarnished status quo into a precious, shiny future. I visualized myself facilitating successful strategic planning meetings when I retired from direct management. I embarked on a personal 47-year quest to understand what the chemistry of strategy was and to develop faster, cheaper, and better processes precisely attuned to needs of the hundreds of thousands of mid-sized, "not-yet-Fortune 500" companies.

The process we followed back in 1976 required weeks of effort to create a strategic plan. That process was a powerful tool for answering the ***what*** and ***why*** questions, but consumed so much of the company's available planning capacity that there wasn't sufficient time left for implementation – i.e., the ***how***. The implementation processes we were following were designed for organizations with the resources of a Fortune 500 company, a club my company was not a member of at the time.

Over 10,000 hours of hands-on facilitation with hundreds of companies and thousands of C-level executives in every sector of the economy led me to develop a bulletproof process for creating, implementing, and sustaining a winning strategy that created and grew value by turning vision into reality. The result is the book you're reading right now.

The Chemistry of Growth documents solutions to the most common strategic and tactical issues you're likely to face as you grow your company. Both the importance of the issues and the effectiveness of the solutions have been field-proven. *Every* smaller business will face these issues as it grows. You will benefit from my experience with companies in a broad range of industries, including energy, finance, food service, government, insurance, legal, logistics, manufacturing, market research, medical, technology, and what I like to call the "intentional nonprofits." This diversity of client companies and the creative approaches they've deployed provide opportunities for cross fertilization. For example, medical practices can benefit from the quality systems that manufacturing firms routinely deploy. Manufacturing firms can benefit from the risk management insights of financial planning firms. And every firm can benefit from the innovation concepts of idea-generating firms.

Who this book is for

I wrote this book for you, if you already are, plan to be, or should be an executive of one of the hundreds of thousands of small to mid-sized companies with 20 to 500 employees. These not-yet-Fortune 500 companies are typically transitioning from the entrepreneur's "back-of-the-envelope" style of management to a professional form of management.

In my experience, small business executives come to the table with different sets of strengths, weaknesses, and experience. *The Chemistry of Growth* speaks to executives and future executives, no matter what their path to executive leadership. You and your fellow executives are likely to fit into one of these profiles:

Alpha wolves from finance, sales, production or development are terrific at working in their specialty. They usually haven't had the need for broader management experience or for worrying about a strategic vision. *The Chemistry of Growth* provides an effective way for these managers to broaden their business perspective with an easy-to-grasp model of strategic vision.

Company founders can usually manage quite effectively on the back of an envelope in the early years. The company's initial strategic focus is acquiring a set of customers, learning how to service them, and surviving long enough to make the next payroll. With growth, the time arrives when the company has sufficient resources and leadership demands to support an executive team. *The Chemistry of Growth* provides insights on how to develop and make effective use of what often becomes the organization's most expensive asset – the executive leadership team.

Former executives of major Fortune 500 companies have experience and understand the value of proven concepts like strategic planning, continuous improvement, and employee development. Unfortunately, the processes they utilized in multi-billion-dollar firms don't scale successfully to small companies. Such large-company processes usually assume the existence of a large department to implement and sustain planning, with levels of headcount and expertise that either don't make sense for, or aren't accessible to, mid-sized companies. *The Chemistry of Growth* provides tools that managers can use to implement their Fortune 500-gained strategic insights without requiring Fortune 500-scale resources.

Freshly-minted MBAs may have little hands-on experience, but plenty of solid book knowledge, albeit often based on their schools' favored Fortune 500 case studies. The pragmatic approaches in *The Chemistry of Growth* can help such managers apply that academic knowledge into career-building practice.

INTRODUCTION

The next generation that will take the reins of the family business. Often the next generation's experience is limited to time spent in the family business. *The Chemistry of Growth* provides insights from multiple industries and companies and a strategic planning process that has proven to be a useful tool in facilitating that transition to the next generation.

Why this book?

This pragmatic book is a tool to help you:

- understand *what* role strategy and strategic planning can and should play in your company;
- understand *why* you would want to utilize the chemistry of growth to dramatically increase the value of your organization and your personal success; and
- acquire practical, proven methodologies that are *how* a small to mid-sized company can develop, implement, and sustain a strategic management process that creates and grows stakeholder value.

This book offers you something hard to find in today's most popular business books: a practical, tested perspective and a strategic process that works for the legions of companies that don't have the resources of an Apple, Amazon, or Toyota. You will gain a deep understanding of *what* strategic management is; *why* it's critical to your organization and your own success; and *how* to create, implement, and sustain a strategy that literally turns vision into reality addressing every organization's mission to create and grow value.

> **This book uses actual, real company examples to illustrate the various elements of the chemistry of growth.**

Over the course of my career, I've experienced myriad challenges and more than my fair share of less-than-optimal decisions. One of my life's goals is to help as many people as possible to avoid these mistakes. I've focused my "lessons" on:

- Addressing the actual issues faced by the majority of small and mid-sized businesses. These are companies – and many divisions within Fortune 500 firms – with anywhere from 20 to 500 employees, all facing significant business challenges that are very different from the issues of the Fortune 500 giants.
- Drawing on the actual experiences of hundreds of different organizations, rather than on just a handful of companies.
- Documenting simple, field-proven processes to address the most common issues. These are "KISS" (Keep It Simple, Stupid) processes that don't assume or require large staffs to implement.

This book uses actual, real company examples to illustrate the various elements of the chemistry of growth. I have changed the names of colleagues, companies and their employees to honor their request for anonymity. In some cases, the experiences of more than one company have been combined to highlight a concept.

I invite you to explore the Chemistry of Growth. Gain a deep understanding of *what* strategy excellence is; *why* it's critical to your organization and your own success; and *how* to create, implement, and sustain a strategy. Learn how to apply a practical, tested perspective and process that works for companies like yours, and you will be able to turn your own vision into reality.

Chapter 1

The Chemistry of Growth

"Nothing great is created suddenly, any more than a bunch of grapes or a fig. If you tell me that you desire a fig, I answer you that there must be time. Let it first blossom, then bear fruit, then ripen."

Epictetus

"...one or two atoms can convert a fuel to a poison, change a color, render an inedible substance edible, or replace a pungent odor with a fragrant one. That changing a single atom can have such consequences is the wonder of the chemical world."

P. W. Atkins

My first strategic planning meeting in 1976 was a defining moment for me and my company. One of the joys of facilitating strategic planning is that I help create such defining moments for others. Sprinkled throughout this book are real company examples from such moments. Here's an example of the power of visualizing a future.

In the first strategic planning meeting with a new market research client, I asked the CEO a follow-up question. "Why do you think customers can be so stupid?" We were elaborating on one of the key weaknesses the executive team had just identified. The weakness was that the market research firm's customers didn't do a good job of implementing, or in many cases, even listening to their recommendations. The CEO had complained: "They use us to find white space in the market, unsatisfied market needs they could exploit with new growth products. Then they drop the ball when it's time to *act* on those insights. Think how much more valuable our research would be if we could find a way to have our recommendations truly implemented."

The CFO then spoke up and asked the "dumb" question: "Why can't we take responsibility for implementing the new product development phase? We already do half the work when we come up with our recommendations, which, by the way, we give away for free along with the research results." Why, indeed?

The strategic planning team responded by creating a strategy, visualizing a future where their company was positioned as the Fortune 500 C-level executives' "go to" source for innovation and growth, rather than merely market research. They strategically remixed the basic elements of their market research business to become that visualized company within five years. They had always had *operational excellence*. What they added now was *strategic excellence*.

Within a few years they became an industry leader, ultimately attracting the attention of a multi-billion-dollar market research firm seeking help to make the same transition globally. They are now implementing their strategy on a global stage as part of that multi-billion dollar organization.

Chapter focus

This chapter discusses how to build a strategy to create your desired future, based on asking and answering three basic questions. **What** do you want the future to look like? **Why** do you want that future? **How** do you get there? The most effective strategy leverages "strategic laws," including the Drucker Phenomenon, the 80/20 Rule, the Experience Curve, the Law of Concentrations, the Law of Critical Mass, the Product Life Cycle, and the Risk/Reward Trade-Off.

The chemistry of growth

The process of successfully growing an organization is like mixing chemicals together to create a reaction. Ask the typical executive to name the most valuable tool in the process of creating a chemical reaction, and they'll offer such answers as the quantity of certain chemicals, the quality of the lab facility, the combination of two or more elements, and so on. That's because we tend to be so rooted in tactical thinking that we miss the larger equation.

The reality is that the most important tool in creating the desired chemical reaction – or growing a company – is the formula that describes its "big picture" results. Without this, a CEO might just as well tell the executive team to grow the company blindfolded. The way to remove the blindfold is to first build a shared, team-supported visualization of where the company wants to be at a given point in the future. This shared visualization is at the heart of the chemistry of growth – where elements in just the right proportions are applied at just the right time (as in a chemical reaction). This visualization provides a company with answers to the basic strategy issues of growth, sustainability, risk, and productivity.

There are three key elements in what I call the chemistry of growth, all critical for effectively communicating a strategy throughout an organization *beyond* the executive team and for the purpose of actually *achieving* that shared vision.

In the chemistry of growth, it is more important to be asking the right questions than to be worrying about the specific answers to those questions. In one of the first companies where I served as the turnaround CEO, I brought in venture capitalists. My liaison with the venture capital firm would randomly show up and drive me crazy with dozens of questions about *what* results we were aiming for, *why* we thought they were worth focusing on, and *how* we expected to accomplish them. With all the passion he exhibited in asking the questions, I never had the sense that he really listened to my answers. In retrospect, I came to appreciate that he knew that making sure that I had asked myself and my executive team these questions was more important than the details of the answers to these questions.

(What + Why + How) ➡ The Future

The primary formula for growth is simple enough:

(What + Why + How) ➡ *The Future*

- *What* do you want your company to look like in the future?
- *Why* do you want it to look like that?
- *How* do you get there?

Strategy is the collective set of answers to those questions of *what*, *why*, and *how*. Strategy answers the above three questions for next week, next month, next quarter, next year, five years, and beyond. For instance:

What executive team today, next year, and five years from today will lead you to that future? Reaching the future requires changing the status quo and implementing that change depends on sustained leadership. Leadership starts with a healthy executive team capable of not only setting the direction but also having the passion and competence to sustain the implementation to get there.

What focus do you want and need? What market and product focus will be sufficient to gain and sustain a competitive advantage through the power of the Experience Curve? (The Experience Curve is a strategic law that recognizes that for most activities, every time you complete an action, you learn how to reduce the cost of the next one.)

What growth do you want and need to achieve your visualization of the future? Growing the value of the organization is the number one challenge for C-level executives like the CEO and CFO.

What organizational changes will be required to reach and sustain your future?

What personnel chemistry will foster engagement, empowerment, and accountability? Strategy memos and PowerPoint presentations won't implement your strategy, your people will.

What productivity gains will be required to sustain a competitive advantage? Every year you, your customers, and your competitors have twelve months to get smarter. A competitor that gets smarter faster than you do ends up winning.

What risks will you have to manage in the future? As you grow, you can and must handle opportunities with higher value. Along with the higher value comes a higher risk. The greater the risk you can effectively manage, the greater the long-term value you can create.

What systems will sustain implementation of your strategy?

What time frames should you set for your expectations? Exploitation of current market and product positions could yield results within a few quarters. Exploration of markets with the potential to totally replace current ones could take years to make a measurable impact.

Strategic laws

A few "strategic laws" underlie the chemistry of growth. Let's take a minute to review these before we move ahead.

The Drucker Phenomenon states that doing the right things adequately will always produce better outcomes than doing the wrong things well.

The Experience Curve states that every time you repeat a transaction you learn how to do it better. For example, studies have shown that every time a manufacturer doubles their production of a specific part, productivity increases between 10 and 25 percent.

The Law of Concentrations states that every connection makes that connection point more attractive for future connections. For example, in social networking, the more followers you have, the more followers you are likely to attract. In business, since it's easier and less risky to purchase from a known vendor, over time a company can find the majority of its revenue coming from a small number of very large customers, with the potential for catastrophic impact should one or two of them leave for any reason.

The Law of Critical Mass states that there is a point when business activity acquires self-sustaining viability. For example, being a market leader can enable you to be the "low cost" provider, provide you with better insight into emerging customer needs, and enable you to set the industry standards for price and features. (Strategically, having the lowest costs allows you to set the market price. None of your competitors can win a price war since you can discount prices below their ability to make a profit.)

The Pareto Principle, also known as the **80/20 Rule**, states that 20 percent of something usually accounts for 80 percent of the results. For example, if you focus on the top 20 percent of your customers you can affect 80 percent of your revenue. This law is recursive; that is, even the 20 percent of the 20 percent (4 percent) is responsible for 80 percent of the 80 percent (64 percent).

The Product Life Cycle states that over time all products move through the four stages of introduction, growth, maturity, and decline. It enables you to estimate when you need to begin the introduction of a new product whose revenue will replace that of one soon moving from maturity to decline. The investment strategy required during the introduction stage would be wildly inappropriate for a product in its declining stage.

The Risk/Reward Trade-Off is an investment theory that correlates an increase in certain types of risk with greater return on an investment. (Lower-risk investments typically yield smaller returns.) For example, you may open a fancy new office in Portland to service the local market with an expectation that the monthly operating costs will be covered within six months by new Portland-area customers. Your greatest risk may be that you have to cover another year of monthly operating losses if it actually takes eighteen months or more to develop that business base.

Strategic processes

The chemistry of growth also relies on a few simple processes that you will use repeatedly over time.

- The qualifying of opportunities by asking and answering: *Is it real? Can we do it? Can we win?* and *Is it worth it?*
- The repetition of asking and answering: *What? Why?* And *How?*
- The strategic planning process of asking and answering of these questions:

  Where are we now?

  Where do we want to be in the future?

  How do we change the status quo to get there?
- The use of team meetings called "swarming" that keeps the team on track. Swarming is a productive team meeting used to quickly complete an *assessment* of where you are, reach *agreement* on the next steps, agree on personal *accountability*, and define the next *actions* to be completed.

In the next chapter, we will discuss what it takes to build a healthy leadership team. If you add up the total compensation of your executive leadership team, you may discover that, as at many other small companies, this is by far your most expensive asset. Improving the effectiveness of this team has an immediate impact on the effectiveness of the organization. Developing and implementing a growth strategy, no matter how brilliant, is impossible without the right leadership.

CHAPTER SUMMARY
The Chemistry of Growth

What are the major concepts in this chapter?

- Building a strategy to create your future is based on asking and answering three basic questions. *What* do you want the future to look like? *Why* do you want that future? *How* do you get there?

- There are "strategic laws," or underlying principles, that your strategy should take advantage of and which affect your ability to implement. These include the Drucker Phenomenon, the Pareto Principle (aka 80/20 Rule), the Experience Curve, the Law of Concentrations, the Law of Critical Mass, the Product Life Cycle, and the Risk/Reward Trade-Off.

Why are these major concepts important?

- The scientific approach of combining the elements of strategy while understanding the underlying strategic laws leads to a better future more quickly.

How can you apply these major concepts?

- Utilize a productive team implementation process based on holding meetings to quickly complete an *assessment* of where you are, reach *agreement* on the next steps, agree on personal *accountability*, and define the next *action* to be completed.

- Utilize a proven strategic planning process that takes place in the course of one- to two-day meetings and that asks and answers the strategic questions. *Where are we now? Where do we want to be in the future? How do we change the status quo to get there?*

- Utilize the "strategic laws" when setting strategies for focus, growth, risk, and time frames.

Want more? Download a FREE workbook at myrna.com/books

Chapter 2

The Chemistry of an Executive Leadership Team

"Good leadership consists of showing average people how to do the work of superior people."

John D. Rockefeller

"Why do you try to form a team? Because teamwork builds trust and trust builds speed."

Russel Honoré

"I'm frustrated with the tension and disconnect I see between my executives, John. I'm hoping that getting them together to build a strategic plan can solve my problem." Bill was the CEO, owner, and founder of Friction PR, a very successful public relations firm. He had just signed a major new client and was worried that their own internal executive friction could prove disastrous.

We scheduled the two-day strategic planning meeting for a Friday and Saturday at a local hotel, a neutral off-site location. However, the negative chemistry of the executive team would prove to pose multiple challenges, as you'll see shortly.

THE CHEMISTRY OF GROWTH

> **Chapter focus**
>
> Successful strategy requires healthy executive team chemistry. This chapter discusses the importance of developing an effective five- to twelve-member leadership team with a balance of competing passions and sufficient strategic and tactical business understanding to shape strategy. It explores ways to develop mutual trust, strategic leadership, and teamwork.

Team chemistry

A healthy executive team is one in which each member:

- provides strategic leadership, effectively communicating what the strategy is, why that is the strategy, and coaching people on how to implement it.
- starts every discussion and decision by asking themselves what's best for the company.
- trusts each other's character, competence, and caring.
- understands, supports and defends each other, not only within the team but outside it.

> **An effective strategic planning process will build and strengthen healthy executive team development and chemistry.**

An effective strategic planning process will build and strengthen healthy executive team development and chemistry. A poor one will damage or destroy team chemistry.

Bill's company had one of the unhealthiest executive teams I'd encountered.

At the first strategic planning meeting I facilitated for Friction PR, the worst eight of negative strategy meeting behavioral archetypes showed up.[1]

- The Absentee
- The CEO (as in Chief Executive Omniscience)
- The Consultant
- The Frog
- The Politician
- The Provocateur
- The Sectarian
- The Theorist

Let's look more closely at each of these negative meeting archetypes one by one.

The Absentee – the individual who is present physically but "somewhere else" mentally. Manuel's head was bent down to stare at his smart phone while he read and responded to emails. He would periodically step out to take or make a phone call. At best, he was half-listening to the discussions, only contributing when asked to comment. Even after I drew the line and insisted that every cell phone, pager, and iPad had to be turned off, Manuel appeared to spend most of his time mentally focused on things happening outside the meeting. (He was staring into space, had us repeat the question whenever he was called on for an opinion, and filled his notepad with stuff unrelated to the discussion at hand.)

Manuel was not invited the next time the executive team met to plan strategically. He was strictly a tactical thinker and Bill needed strategic thinkers for these meetings. Eventually, Bill ended up transferring executive management of Manuel's department to a true executive, allowing Manuel to focus on what he did best – operational excellence.

The CEO – the leader acting in his "Chief Executive Omniscience" mode. Most CEOs are highly intelligent and very intuitive, able to quickly anticipate where any discussion is heading and likely to supply a conclusion to save everybody

---

[1] A note about lists. Too often people ascribe unintended meaning to lists. For example, most people will assume that the first name in a distribution list is more "important" than the last name. I use a simple convention. If the order isn't important, I sort the list alphabetically – as is the case for this list.

the time of figuring it out for themselves. Bill fit this profile and acted just this way. Unfortunately, whenever the team had reached a conclusion this way in the past, team members saw it as Bill's decision rather than their own. Whenever an implementation issue came up, they put the monkey on Bill's back to "fix his decision." In addition, like many entrepreneur CEOs, Bill was notorious for the sheer volume of topics he could raise in one meeting, intermixing the major strategic with the minor tactical. Over time, the executive team members had unconsciously tuned out the noise, which ended up sounding like "blah, blah, bonus, blah, blah, fired, blah, blah, blah…"

I had to enforce the rule that in every discussion during this two-day strategic planning meeting, the CEO would speak last. This enabled Bill to judge how well people truly understood the points of view he had communicated in the past. When Bill did speak, everyone listened intently, since they understood he would be providing new information or correcting a misconception.

Bill's participation in the planning meeting was essential. Actively listening to the discussions enabled him to understand not only **what** the team members wanted to accomplish but **why**. He was more supportive of the resulting strategic plan because he knew what alternatives had been considered. While not initially comfortable in the role, he acted as a participant rather than a problem-solving, time-saving omniscient individual.

The Consultant – the individual who never commits to a team-developed decision. Every time it looked like a decision was about to be made, Ed would pipe up with a comment like "Let me play devil's advocate and outline how we could fail." As if the devil needed an advocate to restate obvious hurdles that everyone in the room already recognized! This would put him in a winning position no matter the ultimate outcome. If the decision turned out to be successful, he would enjoy the triumph of having been part of the team. If it should fail, he could say, "I warned you we shouldn't do that."

I short-circuited this lack of accountability by making it clear that there never is 100% information or certainty when you make a strategic decision, but it's necessary to make a decision and commit to following through. Ed was forced to go on record as supporting the decision. Remember, a strategic plan is not a plan until the executive team leaves the meeting with consensus and commitment. (Consensus means that even if a team member might have made a different decision if it were left entirely up to him, he agrees that it makes sense for the organization and he will commit to support it.)

The Frog – the individual who is so new to the organization that they and the team assume they have nothing to contribute. They expect to listen much and contribute little. However, new employees, especially those who have been on board less than 90 days, are a valuable asset. I like to call them "fresh frogs," based on the old wives' tale about how a frog dropped into a pot of boiling water will jump out, but a frog put into lukewarm water that is slowly heated up will become a cooked frog. Extending the metaphor to the corporate world, the other members of the executive team have been in the pot for years and may not even realize the water is boiling.

I asked Marcos, "What is the stupidest thing you saw when you joined the company?" When he paused to ponder this question, I piped up, to the team's laughter, "The list is so long, he's trying to pick the most important one." I explained to the team that when you interact with a fresh frog, you need to resist the urge to quickly explain things. It's more valuable to ask the fresh frog, "***Why*** do you ask that question, ***what*** do you see that we don't?" After that, the other team members would stop and listen attentively whenever Marcos spoke up.

The Politician – the individual who tells everyone a different story behind closed doors. Jack tells Joe, "Just between us, Jolene is an idiot and I don't have any confidence in her ability." He tells Jolene, "Just between us, I don't believe Joe appreciates your hard work." He avoids any meetings where Joe and Jolene would hear the same story from him. The Friday morning of the planning meeting, Jack actually phoned in to say he wouldn't be attending since he had finally scheduled a sales meeting at the Mexican consulate. Bill told him to get his sorry butt back to the company meeting. Strategic planning was important stuff and he wasn't buying Jack's story that the meeting with the consulate had to be held now.

I prodded Jack during the strategic planning meeting to respond with substance. His backup strategy (if he couldn't tell everyone a different story) was to try to get away with issuing meaningless platitudes when speaking in front of the entire team. He found he couldn't sustain his political behavior when he was constantly forced to go on record in front of everybody.

The Provocateur – the individual who never considers an issue closed, a discussion concluded, or a decision final. As often as not, when the group accepts his passionately made suggestion, he immediately comes out against it. He appears committed to perpetuating a frenzy of uncertainty and inaction. On the second day of the strategic planning meeting, the Friction PR executive team began to set the agreed-upon strategy to paper. Julian, this team's provocateur, immediately tried to reopen each decision. "The strategy has us growing too fast. The targeted profit margin is too low. How will we develop new products when we can't even get today's products working?" On and on he went.

> **Never do something stupid because of something written on a sheet of paper. The written strategy is a communications tool, not a license to do stupid things.**

Patiently but firmly, I reminded Julian of the pledge he and the rest of the team had taken at the start of the meeting: "We will never do something stupid because of something written on a sheet of paper. The written strategy is a communications tool, not a license to do stupid things." I reinforced the chemistry of growth formula of *what* we want the future to look like, *why* we want that future, and *how* we change the status quo to achieve that future. "We can't begin moving in a direction until we decide where we want to end up," I said. "Rather than flailing, we will make adjustments along the way. Asking and answering *how* is what action planning is all about. This is the next step after providing answers to the questions of *what* and *why*." Over time, Julian was able to productively channel his energy into making sure conflicting viewpoints were aired while accepting and embracing the team's ultimate decisions.

The Sectarian – the individual who sees their role as only representing the thoughts of their function, department, and/or people. Caroline, the Human Resources Director, saw her role as representing HR, and only HR. Whenever the discussion turned to areas other than HR, such as sales, production, or finance, she tuned out. She didn't understand that her experience, insights, and perspective were valuable and required to shape the optimal strategy for the company.

I pushed her out of her comfort zone, requiring her to comment on each issue discussed. This drew her into the overall strategy development. As it turned out, she triggered one of the meeting's "aha" moments when she commented on a production issue from her perspective.

The Theorist – the individual who won't be around in three to five years to live with the consequences of the team's strategic decisions. (As Lucius Annaeus Seneca pointed out over 2,000 years ago, "Be wary of the man who urges an action in which he himself incurs no risk.") This team had two theorists, Jill and Patrick. Jill had recently tendered her resignation, planning to move to a new company at the first of the new year. She had been invited to the planning meeting because of her expertise. She pushed back whenever we discussed any strategy that would require investments this year that could impact her year-end bonus. Patrick was a business colleague of Bill's who served on the board of advisors and who kept pushing for risky strategies he had read about in the *Harvard Business Review* that could make the company millions – in the unlikely case that they would work for Friction PR. Failure would have no impact on Patrick, since he had no skin in the game.

At the end of the first day of the planning meeting, at my suggestion, Bill excused them both from attending the second day, since they wouldn't be accountable for the implementation or suffer any consequences from a poor strategy. The takeaway lesson here is that your strategic planning team shouldn't include "lame ducks."

Building the executive team

Building a healthy executive team is a process. There is no magical alchemist's stone that will do it. I've observed that team-building programs that are external to the work environment, like popular "ropes courses," have limited impact. Too often attendees have told me that the behaviors learned in the woods *stay* in the woods and everyone reverts to the same old way of acting the next day. As with strategic planning, those team-building programs that integrate with the day-to-day execution of the business have proven to be far more effective.

Building personal relationships through the development and execution of strategy builds a healthy executive team. Working with hundreds of teams has led me to an understanding of the chemistry of success for strategic planning meetings. Here are the approaches proven to work:

> **Strategic meetings need a large block of uninterrupted time with flexible ending times.**

Define the meeting type: Separate strategic meetings from tactical/operational meetings. Operational meetings need to have firm ending times so as not to impact other scheduled commitments. Strategic meetings need a large block of uninterrupted time with flexible ending times. You don't want to be close to having worked through a major issue or decision when a team member has to leave to catch a flight.

Limit members: Limit the total number of team members in strategic planning meetings to between five and twelve people. With fewer than five, you don't have sufficient heads in the business; over twelve and the dynamics of strategic discussions and decision-making break down.

Change members periodically: Have the fortitude to change the composition of the executive and planning team over time. Internal and external changes will periodically require new expertise and insights. This is a working group, and membership is not a reward for longevity at the company. Every member should have the attitude and aptitude to contribute to the strategic direction. Thinking strategically doesn't come naturally to everyone, so allow sufficient time for people to sync with the requirements. However, once it's clear that this is not the right role for someone, replace that person with someone who is better suited.

Use a facilitator: Always utilize a skilled meeting facilitator for strategic meetings. An external facilitator who commands respect, enforces the rules, and has the ability to move the group to consensus is essential. Facilitating is a full-time job that doesn't leave someone with the time to be a full participant in the strategy discussions. Thus, the CEO should never be the facilitator.

Clarify roles: Clarify the roles of participants and the CEO. The role of the participants is to look at every issue as if they are the CEO; i.e., to focus on what's best for the organization as a whole rather than themselves, their people, or their function. The CEO's role is to shut up and first listen to all the members before stepping in to dot the I's and cross the T's.

Follow rules: Demand that members follow this set of rules for productive meetings:

1. Listen actively.
2. Speak up and say what needs to be said – there are no sacred cows.
3. Focus on solving problems rather than placing blame or being defensive.
4. Respect differences of opinion.
5. Avoid cheap shots.
6. Stay focused.
7. Add only new information to the discussion. Don't flog a dead horse.
8. Permit only one discussion at a time.
9. Silence implies understanding and agreement.
10. Finish with consensus and commit to action.

Let's look at each of these ten rules in a little more detail.

Rule 1: Listen actively

George Bernard Shaw is quoted as having said, "England and America are two countries separated by a common language." This is an even more dramatic condition between the various professionals in a company. For example, accountants attach a different meaning to the word "revenue" than salespeople do. (In fact, I've heard at least six different definitions in planning meetings.) Computer programmers use the phrase "finished" differently than anyone else.

I once said, "I believe in participatory management. I think we all should manage that way." My colleague's quick response was, "You're wrong! I don't believe in making a decision by voting, that is an abrogation of leadership." I had to clarify that I meant that I believed everyone affected by a decision should have the opportunity to provide their thoughts and insights before I made a decision. I still had the responsibility to *make* the decision, just one that was better informed and more likely to be supported by people who were respected enough to have their opinions solicited ahead of time.

Listening requires an interactive dialogue to make sure that people actually understand what is being said. Active listening generates questions such as "*What* do you mean when you say quality is poor? Give me some examples." "*Why* do you think we need an office in London? Who would be the customer?"

Rule 2: Speak up and say what needs to be said – there are no sacred cows

"Why do we pay a premium for being the first to purchase the newest piece of hardware?" Sally asked in the first strategic planning meeting she was invited to attend at Scientific Processing. The predominantly technical executive team was appalled by her question. One of the engineers' responses was representative: "We are a technology-driven company. Our customers expect us to have the latest hardware. Why even ask the question?"

Sally persisted. "But we don't seem to have time to utilize any of the new features for at least two years. Wouldn't it be better to purchase a used machine two years later when it sells for a much, much lower price?" Putting that "sacred cow" issue on the table ended up helping the company move from losing money every month to making money every month. Shortly after the meeting ended, they replaced their spanking-new hardware with used equipment that cost thousands of dollars less, without negatively affecting their customers. All because Sally, a non-engineer, had asked "*why*?"

Rule 3: Focus on solving problems rather than placing blame or being defensive

Sales knows exactly what the problem is: "If Bob and his crew in production would get off their butts and deliver what we sold, everything would be fine." Bob's response was just as simple and nonproductive. "If the damn salespeople would focus on selling what we can produce instead of making stuff up, everything would be fine." Wasting time with the two departments blaming each other didn't get the company any closer to solving the problem of a poorly defined product line. Of course there are problems. The only time a company doesn't have challenges is when it's in a stagnant market or not growing. One of the signs of a healthy executive team is how little time is wasted on placing blame and being defensive.

Rule 4: Respect differences of opinion

Each team member brings a different perspective to the table, which is important because strategic issues usually touch multiple functions of the company. An optimal strategy benefits from a 360-degree view of each strategic issue. Bert, the controller, was bragging a bit about how he had improved the company's cash flow by shifting payment of vendors from 30 days to 60 days. "You'd be amazed how much that's added to our bottom line." Carol, the head of production, responded: "Oh? Can that be the reason our vendors no longer give us priority treatment when we need a rush shipment of raw materials? Do you have any idea how much it costs us to priority ship because we had to wait for raw materials?"

The ideal leadership team is a diverse team with members of different ages, with different life and business experiences, different affinities with customers and vendors, and different passions. You must respect the differences of opinion to realize the value of that diversity. (You show respect when you solicit, understand, and consider the opinions of people affected by your decisions *before* you make them.)

Business is complex and it isn't possible to literally know it all. In addition to their leadership team, top performing CEOs belong to a CEO peer group like Vistage, enabling them to benefit from the insights and perspectives of a diverse mix of CEOs who have been there and done that.

Rule 5: Avoid cheap shots

Beyond the obvious negative effects, cheap shots in a meeting can be used to short-circuit decision making. Often, as the team discusses a long-standing issue, a consensus begins to emerge on the action to take. A decision to act, however, will generate additional work and requires personal accountability. It's fun to discuss a problem as long as you never commit to a solution. When it appears that this time the team is actually converging on taking action, a cheap shot is an effective way to derail the discussion and save everyone from the necessary extra work that a decision would create. The cheap shot-taker can then sit back and think: "Dodged a bullet! I can go back to work as usual and not worry about adding that task to my already burdened work day."

> **If you chase two rabbits, both will escape. Strategic planning meetings are about deciding which are the right things to do.**

Rule 6: Stay focused

An ancient proverb warns: "If you chase two rabbits, both will escape." Strategic planning meetings are about deciding which are the right things to do. The team needs to focus on what's most important or the things that will show greater return. Joe Mancuso, founder of the CEO Clubs, retells the story of how one of his CEO members decided to save money and facilitate the strategic planning meeting himself. "He and the team spent half the time talking about the lack of toilet paper in the women's bathrooms and never did get to discuss their truly strategic issues." Without strategic focus you will end up going down a rabbit hole while both rabbits escape.

Rule 7: Add only new information to the discussion. Don't flog a dead horse

"Everything would be better if only we had more salespeople." Omari was like a broken record. Every ten minutes he would go off on why having more salespeople was important. "Everything would be better if only we had more salespeople." Then ten minutes later, "Everything would be better if..." Finally, someone spoke up and said, "Does everybody understand that Omari feels 'everything would be better if only we had more salespeople'? We don't need to bring that up again." This rule doesn't prevent the team from bringing up an issue they have discussed in the past. It just says they don't need to use up air time repeating it over and over again.

Rule 8: Permit only one discussion at a time

It should go without saying that you can't listen while you're talking. No, you can't listen actively when you're having a private conversation with the person sitting next to you. You aren't fully engaged when you're reading and responding to the emails or texts on your smart phone.

Rule 9: Silence implies understanding and agreement

It's three months after the strategic planning meeting, and the CEO wants to know why Chuck hasn't implemented his action steps. "Well, I never agreed with that decision," Chuck protests. The CEO says in exasperation, "But you were in the meeting and a member of the team. Why didn't you speak up then?" Chuck shrugs his shoulders.

Life is too short to allow this to happen. Make it clear to everyone on the executive team that they must speak up on a timely basis or forever hold their peace.

Yolanda also hasn't implemented as planned. When asked why she agreed to something she didn't believe in, her answer was instructive. "I didn't understand what you guys were talking about, so I just went with the crowd." The CEO asks, "Then why didn't you ask for an explanation?" Yolanda replies: "Well, I was hesitant to waste everybody's time asking what cash flow was. I thought everyone assumed I would understand since I was on the team."

The fact is, business is complicated and few people can understand every aspect of it. A healthy executive team appreciates this and has no problem pausing to allow one member to provide a short tutorial from their area of expertise.

Rule 10: Finish with consensus and commit to action

At the end of every discussion ask, "What's next?" Create, document, and then follow up on an action step that includes who's accountable for the action and when that action step has to be completed.

Enforcing the rules

Enforcing these rules is crucial and can usually be best performed by the outside facilitator. (When I facilitate meetings I empower everyone to be a referee by actually giving everyone a physical yellow "foul flag" they can toss at the offender. It's a good way to enforce rules because anyone can flag an inappropriate comment in a light-hearted, yet effective, way.)

Let's explore how these rules, and the overall process, support essential team relationships and healthy executive team chemistry.

The importance of intimacy

The strongest teams develop a sense of, to use a somewhat provocative word, intimacy. Intimacy is established when you make yourself vulnerable and share something that would be potentially embarrassing if shared with others. A healthy executive team can be open about personal goals, weaknesses, and objectives. They know that their team members will never use that information to hurt them, but will keep it private. They will use those intimate details to better support each other. We periodically ask each executive to share where they want to be in five years. On the healthiest teams, each executive will openly share their personal goals. On dysfunctional teams, they tend to provide empty answers, such as "I want to be doing a good job doing what's best for the company."

The importance of trust

The chemistry of a healthy executive team requires that team members trust each other. Trust is built on the three C's: character, competence, and caring.

There is nothing a team can't accomplish when they can trust each member to have:

- *Character*: honestly sharing the good and the bad.
- *Competence*: knowing what they are best at and seeking help with what they want to improve.
- *Caring*: understanding and considering what is important to each of their teammates, their company, and their customers.

Bill, the CEO we met at the start of this chapter, focused on building Friction PR's executive leadership team and it paid handsome dividends. He replaced several executives with strategic thinkers. He held everyone accountable for behaviors that were consistent with the meeting rules and roles. They leveraged their new client to change the status quo and put the company on a clear path to turn their vision into reality and experience exceptional growth.

> **A healthy executive team requires a mix of counterbalancing advocates.**

The invisible chemistry

There is one additional characteristic of a healthy executive leadership team, diversity of passions.

Gary was at it again. "We need to order the additional press now or we will be unable to meet our commitment to customers later this year." The team members nodded their heads. Gary was always pushing to increase capacity at Specialty Printing, the company where he worked. The CFO turned his attention to the Sales VP: "Our VP of Manufacturing wants us to invest another $1.5 million dollars, is the pipeline strong enough to warrant that?" After reviewing the current and expected business, the decision was made this time to place the order. This was a fortunate choice, as the company would otherwise have been crushed by the surge of new business that arrived later that year.

Gary proved to be a reliable steward, making sure that the company remained able to deliver on its customer commitments. He also developed a very capable second in command, Ben, who took over when Gary retired. Production continued to run smoothly under Ben's leadership, except for one major thing. Ben decided to skip the frustration of constantly having to push for new capacity. He'd just wait until he was asked before proposing any new investments. Finally, about a year after Gary had retired, the company lost two major customers because it suddenly found itself unable to meet their delivery requirements. The team hadn't recognized that when Gary retired, they lost an essential element of their successful chemistry – a passionate advocate for capacity.

A healthy executive team requires a mix of counterbalancing advocates. There must be an advocate constantly pushing for more aggressive growth balanced by an advocate for control and profitability. There should be an advocate pushing to explore new products and technology balanced by another pushing to fully exploit the current ones. Take stock of how the mix of passions changes whenever the membership of your executive team changes. Make sure that the company's decisions don't become too conservative or risky because a counterbalancing voice has been lost.

The next chapter outlines a proven strategic planning process. The planning process can be more important than the plan itself. It's likely that any of the members of the executive leadership team could create a reasonable plan. But, for a plan to be implemented, each member of the leadership team has to understand, agree, and internalize not only **what** the plan is but **why** they're taking this particular course (and not the many possible alternatives). The process is the catalyst that activates the plan.

CHAPTER SUMMARY

The Chemistry of an Executive Leadership Team

What are the major concepts in this chapter?

- Each team member must develop trust in each other's character, competence, and caring.
- Each team member must provide strategic leadership, effectively communicating *what* the strategy is, *why* that is the strategy, and coaching people on *how* to implement it.
- Each team member must understand, support and defend each other within the team and outside it.
- The executive leadership team is also characterized by their balance of competing passions. There must be advocates pushing the strategic themes of growth, risk, sustainability, and productivity.
- The executive leadership team needs to be a balanced group of five to twelve members with sufficient strategic and tactical understanding of the business to shape strategy.

Why are these major concepts important?

- Everybody in the company contributes to success.
- Failure is the exclusive responsibility of leadership. (Doing the right things adequately will always let you outperform those who are doing the wrong things well.)

How can you apply these major concepts?

- Commit to a formal strategic planning process that fosters team development and chemistry. For example, "we will utilize a formal strategic planning process with regular follow-up."
- Identify key new strategic executive positions that need to be filled over the next five years as the company evolves. For

example, "we will recruit/develop senior executives in Finance – CFO, Marketing – CMO, and International Sales."
- Practice what you preach by insisting on following the roles in strategic meetings.

   ### Participants' Role
   1. Look at the organization through the eyes of the CEO.
   2. Represent the organization, not yourself, not your people, not your department, not your function.

   ### CEO's Role
   1. Act as a participant, not as the "omniscient individual."
   2. Suspend your usual problem-solving and "time-saving" operating mode.

- Practice what you preach by insisting on following rules that develop trust, consensus, and commitment in strategic meetings.
- Abide by the ten rules for productive meetings
   1. Listen actively.
   2. Speak up and say what needs to be said – there are no sacred cows.
   3. Focus on solving problems rather than placing blame or being defensive.
   4. Respect differences of opinion.
   5. Avoid cheap shots.
   6. Stay focused.
   7. Add only new information to the discussion. Don't flog a dead horse.
   8. Permit only one discussion at a time.
   9. Silence implies understanding and agreement.
   10. Finish with consensus and commit to action.

Want more? Download a FREE workbook at myrna.com/books

Chapter 3

Team Planning: The Catalyst for Successful Strategy

"Management is doing things right; leadership is doing the right things."

Peter Drucker

"You've got to be very careful if you don't know where you're going, because you might not get there."

Yogi Berra

"Where do you want to be five years in the future?" I was facilitating a first-time strategic planning meeting for a high tech company that had hit a wall.

"That's a question we've never been asked before," Lee, the CEO remarked. The executive team members, being mostly technical people, started calculating. "If we continue to grow at the same rate we have every year, then…"

"No!" I exclaimed. "Where do you **want** to be in the future? I'm not asking for a forecast, projection, or fantasy number." As I went around the table, asking each person in turn to answer the question, we discovered the solution to the mystery of the company's dysfunction. Casey, the director of development, envisioned a small, private, craftsman-like company based in one location. Mark, the director of sales, saw their future as a large, public company with multiple products. Mitchell, the operations manager, visualized multiple manufacturing locations around the world. Jaime, the controller, just wanted the company to be profitable. Every day the executive leadership team was making decisions shaped by their individual visualization of the future, a future where the company was simultaneously big and small, private and public, physically concentrated and spread across the globe. Was it any wonder that as each of these executives drove toward what they thought was a shared vision of the future, they were frustrating another executive driving in the opposite direction?

> **The strategic planning process succeeded in getting every executive pointing in the same direction with profound effect. "Even if nothing else had been accomplished," the CEO told me, "the alignment became a catalyst for execution."**

The strategic planning process succeeded in getting every executive pointing in the same direction with profound effect. "Even if nothing else had been accomplished," the CEO told me, "the alignment became a catalyst for execution." (In chemistry a catalyst is a substance that speeds up a chemical reaction, but is not consumed by the reaction; hence a catalyst can be recovered chemically unchanged at the end of the reaction it has been used to speed up, or catalyze. In business it is someone or something that causes a big change.)

Chapter focus

The strategic planning process that creates the strategic plan is even more important than the plan itself. This chapter outlines how to make strategic planning a sustainable, step-by-step team planning process rather than a random event. It discusses the value of aligning people's personal visualizations of the company's desired future so they reinforce each other and create synergy. It also provides a model that clarifies and links each element of the strategic plan – vision, mission, strategy, and strategic goals – so that the model provides a stable platform from which you can initiate, complete, and realize the rewards of your investments in strategy.

Timelines

Chemical reaction times can vary wildly. Mix barley and yeast with a few additional ingredients, bake for an hour, and you have a loaf of barley bread. Mix barley, yeast, and other ingredients, ferment over a month or more, and you have a mug of beer to enjoy with your bread. If you mix barley and yeast, ferment and distill it, then pour it into a charred white oak cask, in three to thirty-six years you can enjoy a glass of fine whisky.

Similarly, executing different elements of your strategy will produce varied results over different time periods. What you plan to accomplish within the next one to ninety days is tactical. What you plan to accomplish within the next five, ten, or thirty years is strategic. In every case, you need to invest company resources today to achieve your planned results.

Strategic planning organizes and anchors a company's investments in the future. When you make an investment you need a platform that will remain stable long enough to complete the investment and realize the reward. To deliver real results, you need a good strategic business planning process that provides the stable platform for making sure everything you do today is consistent with where you want to be in the future.

The elements of a strategic plan and the Progress Pyramid™

A strategic plan has six basic elements – vision, mission, strategy, strategic goals, key results, and action steps. Each element has a different period of stability. Visualize your plan as a pyramid made up of six stable investment platforms (see The Progress Pyramid™). Tactical initiatives produce a result within days, weeks, or months. They don't require a platform that's stable beyond 90 days.

Why do you invest resources in those short-term tactical initiatives? It's to progress toward achieving strategic results which can take years or decades of investment to achieve. Sustaining those strategic investments long enough to reap a return requires platforms that are stable for years or decades. As such, they must have an equally long stable platform. The written strategic plan documents these six investment platforms, each one stable long enough to enable a return on an investment. We will discuss each level of the plan further in this chapter.

> **The planning process can be more important than the plan itself.**

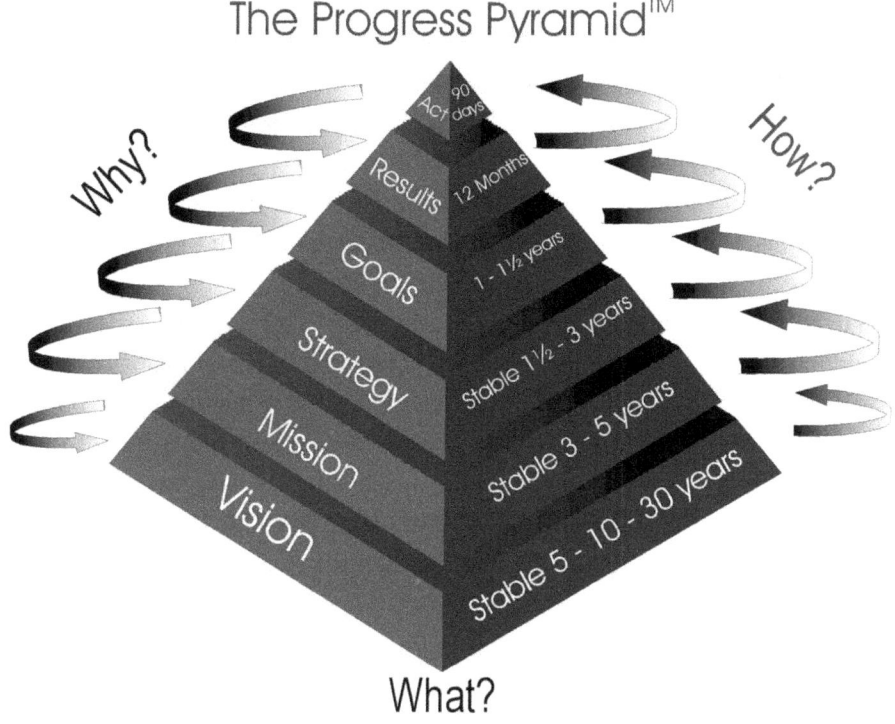

The elements of a strategic planning process

The planning process can be more important than the plan itself. Strategic planning is a continuous process of answering three questions.

- *Where are we now?*
- *Where do we want to be in the future?*
- *What do we need to focus on over the next period to get there?*

Get ready to plan

The planning process starts with establishing the team that will develop the plan. It's unlikely that any single individual, outside expert, consultant, or even the CEO understands all the specifics of your company, market, and technology as well as the team of people who experience it day in and day out. Further, no outsider or single individual will execute your plan. Execution requires a committed team that understands not only *what* they are expected to do, but *why* they must act.

As we've noted earlier in the book, your planning team should have five to twelve members who can look at the business with the eyes of a CEO. A true executive is someone who seeks answers that optimize the entire organization, not just their department, people, or own position. The team should include the owner(s) and their direct reports, heads of major company functions, and one or two employees who will have a major impact on the company's future. Sometimes it makes sense to augment the team with one or two outsiders who have a major stake in the company's success. The team already possesses the knowledge needed to create the plan. If they don't have the specific answers in their heads, they can identify questions to be answered as part of the strategic plan's execution.

The CEO is a key member of the planning team. The three responsibilities a CEO can't delegate are championing the strategic planning process, developing the management team, and making the "bet the company" decisions. These three responsibilities are at the heart of strategic business planning. The planning process provides an opportunity for the CEO to assess the current state of his executive leadership team. By listening to everyone before giving what he considers the "correct answer," the CEO can learn just how well his team understands the issues and existing direction. Interacting this way will ensure he and the plan are aligned while allowing sufficient room for the team to end up truly "owning" the final plan.

> **The most effective environment for creating the plan is a well-facilitated, intense two-day meeting.**

The most effective environment for creating the plan is a well-facilitated, intense two-day meeting. Why two days rather than one or more than two? Disciplining yourself to complete the plan within two days rather than weeks keeps the team's yearly focus on implementation, the hardest part of any plan. Covering all the key company issues in one meeting produces a plan that better balances competing issues such as growth, profitability, and competition. The two-day format puts the team into a "state of flow," where they hold all of the priority issues and their interactions in their heads. Flow is one of the keys to good design. (I discuss the concept of flow in more depth in Chapter 10.) We have found that there can be a significant reduction in the quality of the planning when it is shoehorned into a single day.

There is a natural flow with the overreaching themes of communications, transition, and focus. The theme of the first day is *communications*, getting everyone on the same page and into that state of flow regarding current issues. That evening provides a *transition* time so the team members can absorb and reflect on the day's discussions. The theme of the second day is *focus*, agreeing on overall direction, this year's strategic direction, and the initial tactical action plans to achieve this. Allocating two days has proven to yield effective planning.

At the meetings I facilitate, I ask participants to start at 8 a.m. and be prepared to work into the evening as late as 8 p.m. both days, if warranted. The team's commitment to being available into the evening provides room for the team to dig more deeply into an issue if required. In my experience, about a third of the meetings utilize the extra hours. The "world's record" for an ending time for one of the meetings I've facilitated is 1:30 a.m., with 11:30 p.m. in the number two slot. The point is that your strategic planning meeting is the one time the leadership team gets away from focusing on the trees and really looks at the forest. It is a huge investment to pull that team away from their day-to-day responsibilities. The worst use of that investment would be if one or two key executives have to leave at 4:30 p.m., just as the team was close to resolving one of the company's long-standing issues. While operational meetings must end on time in order for everyone to keep on schedule and meet personal commitments, strategic meetings need to end when the team reaches consensus and commitment.

Let's take a look at the three key questions we started with, one by one. The planning process begins with determining where you are *now*.

Step 1: Where Are We Now?

To identify where your company is now, evaluate your firm's Weaknesses[2], Opportunities, Threats, and Strengths in what's known as the WOTS-up process. Conducting a WOTS-up analysis allows you to identify the major issues facing your company today, and helps the entire team gain a comprehensive understanding of those issues and possible responses.

Before your planning meeting, solicit independent thinking from your team through a structured online, anonymous, input form. Ask for answers to these questions:

- What are the company's five top weaknesses, opportunities, threats, and strengths?
- Where do they personally want to see the company within five years, including major market and product focus?
- What parts of the status quo do they think need to change?

Soliciting prioritized input before the team gets together minimizes the risk of "group think." It also gets the team members to start thinking strategically.

During the planning meeting, utilize handouts consolidated from this input and hold a facilitated discussion around each of the WOTS-up topics. This helps each team member understand everyone's perspective on the most important issues. The key value of this process is the interactive discussions that develop insights.

Document *where you are* with a prioritized list of the dozen or so identified major issues, including a short commentary on each.

Here are some examples of actual strategic issues that triggered game-changing strategies in various companies we've worked with.

$12 million lost business report: Provided the justification for adding additional capacity. There was enough existing business to more than cover the cost!

Aging leadership: Accelerated creation of programs to create a pipeline of younger managers when the team realized that all the company's leaders were

---

[2] Why WOTS-up rather than the more common SWOT analysis? I have found that the discussions around weaknesses are the most productive way to surface company issues. Ending on strengths provides a positive transition to the next planning stage.

from the same generation and would be retiring within a few years of each other.

Competitors selling below cost: Moved the team beyond the apparent stupidity of the competitor to ask and answer the question: "How could they be making money if they sell below cost?" The answer led to a new paradigm for winning incremental "spot market" business based on accurate monthly projections of unused capacity. Incremental business could be bid based on its variable costs once the company covered all the fixed costs.

New product failures: Led to creating an independent new product development team with dedicated sales, marketing, and technical staff. It wasn't realistic to expect new product and market development to get the priority it needed when assigned to staff focused on meeting the real-time demands of current customers. The old approach had produced new products that consistently lacked key features, entered the market months later than their competitors, and were ignored by the sales force.

No new customer wins: Woke the team up to the need to transition to an Internet-based technology on a crash basis once they realized that 100% of revenue growth for the past couple of years came from a declining base of legacy customers who were locked into their current technology.

Poor win-to-bid ratio: Required the revamping of the estimating function to add a stronger qualification step to reduce the number of bids processed. The high volume of bids had led to a killer mix of late responses and shoddy analysis, often adding 25% to the bid price "just in case." With fewer, better qualified bids to respond to, the estimating department had the time to identify lower-cost solutions with a profound impact on the win ratio, especially when the company had been losing bids on price by as little as 5 to 10 percent.

Step 2: Where Do We Want to Be in the Future?

Once you know where you stand today, you can then develop a strategy, mission, and vision for where you want your company to be in the future. Progress is accelerated by making sure that each action you take today keeps you on a path to where you want to be five years and beyond. (Make sure that today's actions are sufficient to help you reach milestones that are a quarter, a year, etc., along the way.) Decide where you want to end up, and then work backward to identify what you should be working on today.

Strategy is the central focus of your plan. Growing your company is like assembling a giant jigsaw puzzle. Imagine you and your team working on the puzzle without the picture on the box. Even worse, suppose there are extra pieces tossed in from other puzzles. Creating, documenting, and communicating a picture of where you want to be within five years gets everybody on the same page. Comparing that picture against where you are today identifies the gaps that you need to focus on closing over the next 18 months.

Your **strategy** should be consistent with your **vision** and **mission**. Think of your **mission** as the DNA of your organization. It is how you've "genetically engineered" your company to survive and thrive in the marketplace. It creates a focus and affirmation of the company you intend to become over the next three to five years. Agree on one or two words or phrases that answer each of the following four questions:

- *What do you want to be?* (Usually some statement of leadership)
- *What customers do you want do it for?* (Usually a statement of geographic scope, industry, targeted customer profile)
- *Why do you do it?* (Usually to *create and grow value* for your customers, employees, and owners along with a "softer" thought like aid the environment, save lives, have fun – if it's true)
- *How do you want to do it?* (Usually some combination of develop, manufacture, supply or market specific services or products)

The words and phrases can be "wordsmithed" into a nice paragraph after the team agrees on the content. It's the content that provides focus.

> **Companies that stand the test of time are anchored with a set of three to five core values shared by all employees and a broad-focusing core purpose beyond "making money."**

TEAM PLANNING: THE CATALYST FOR SUCCESSFUL STRATEGY

Futurist John Naisbitt has cautioned that "Strategic planning is worthless – unless there is first a strategic vision." Your **vision** informs your **mission**. Companies that stand the test of time are anchored with a set of three to five core values shared by all employees and a broad-focusing core purpose beyond "making money." They are inspired by a Big Hairy Audacious Goal[3] that might take ten to thirty years to achieve.

To create your **strategy**, ask yourself and your team where you *want to be* within five years. It is important that everyone understands that they are not being asked for a forecast, projection, or prediction. Document that strategy as specific answers to the following questions: (We delve deeper into these areas later in the book.)

Revenue: How much from internally generated growth, how much from acquisitions, how much from existing clients and products, how much from new?

Profit: EBITDA, gross margin, or pre-tax, and is it before or after items such as bonuses, profit-sharing, 401(k) contributions, charitable donations, etc.?

Acquisitions and partnerships: How many, what size range, is it for revenue, customers, people, additional locations, and/or technology?

Market focus: How many markets, descriptions, adding/dropping, what's each one's share of revenue and profit? How will you reach these markets?

Product focus: How many, descriptions, adding/dropping, what's each one's share of revenue and profit?

Relationships: Vendors, customers, competitors, community?

Customer profiles: How many major customers, how many total customers?

Geography: Your target market, proactively seeking customers – local, regional, national, North America, international, or global? (International implies U.S.-based sales to internationally-based customers, and global implies sales, support and often, production located in the targeted country.)

---

[3] Jim Collins coined the phrase "Big Hairy Audacious Goal" in his classic book *Built to Last*.

Productivity: What are your productivity goals for revenue and profit per employee? How will you utilize automation, outsourcing, globalization, re-engineering?

Organization: Number of full-time equivalent employees to support the business, major job categories, key positions to add, staff development?

Locations: Where are headquarters, new facilities, remote offices?

Technology strategy: Innovator, fast follower, slow adapter, late adapter? The role of the Internet, emerging technologies?

Branding: Under the radar, larger than life, look and feel, promotion?

Risk management: What's the largest acceptable concentration of customer, product, and/or industry revenue?

For the strategy to communicate effectively, it must include specific numbers such as "grow to $15 million with a consistent pretax margin of 12 percent." Vague statements such as "grow larger with a superior profit" aren't meaningful. All numbers should be estimated to the "ballpark" level of accuracy, as close as the team's current knowledge allows.

> **"Is what I'm doing today consistent with getting where we want to be within five years?"**

Accuracy is more important than precision. Whether you say "grow to $15 million," "$30 million" or "$9 million," the numbers are a "ballpark" range that accurately communicate the target. Nobody is going to throw themselves on a spear if the company "only" grows to $13.5 million or it takes six years to hit $15 million. The key is for everyone in the organization to ask themselves a simple question: "Is what I'm doing today consistent with getting where we want to be within five years?" If not, you have one of two choices: change what you're doing today, the usual tactical adjustment, or change where you want to be in the future, the strategic adjustment. Tactical adjustments you can make on your own. Strategic adjustments need to be done by the executive leadership team, usually during the annual strategic planning meeting.

Remember the pledge we began the book with? ("I will never do something stupid because of something written on a sheet of paper.") Why is this so important? It seems that everyone has had the experience of providing a number in good faith and subsequently being clubbed with it months later. Without the above pledge, there is a fear that management will forget the original context for that number and use any specific number as a club. Taking the pledge frees the team to make their strategy statement crystal-clear.

Step 3: What Do We Need to Focus On Over the Next Period to Get There?

Once you know where you are and where you want to go, you can take the third step of matching your **strategy** against the prioritized, understood set of issues that document where you are now. Identify the most important things that must be in place within 18 months in order for the team to be on a path to realizing the strategy – the team's visualization of where they want to be within five years.

Identify four to six major **strategic goals** that cluster the changes in the status quo that will be required to implement and achieve the desired outcomes. Identify a single individual with passion and competence to champion each of the goals. (Champions are usually a member of the leadership team.) The rule of thumb is simple: one **strategic goal** per champion. By definition, an individual can only have one most important **strategic goal**. Developing the goals as a team keeps everyone on the same page. Driving implementation individually makes sure each goal gets priority attention.

Why four to six rather than twelve or only one? Have you ever been in a meeting where you are reviewing twelve items? Was anyone listening after the seventh or eighth item? A strategic plan is a tool for implementing strategy. Ninety percent of a company's resources are typically committed to day-to-day operations, leaving ten percent available at best for strategic investments. Keeping four to six **strategic goals** front and center is a constant challenge. Keeping focus on a dozen **strategic goals** is all but impossible. (Twelve **strategic goals** is an oxymoron.)

Why not one, then? Because one doesn't fully exploit the capacity of your leadership team. The more personal ownership there is of individual elements of the plan, the more likely that element will remain a priority. A thoughtful definition of each **strategic goal** and its **key result measures** will enable you to create and sustain both corporate and individual strategic focus.

Develop an action plan for each **strategic goal**. Action plans are the vehicle for managing execution and achieving the goals. Action plans identify the **strategic goal**, **key results**, champions, and accountable persons. For each **strategic goal**, ask the team to identify the one to seven **key results** that need to be in place within 12 months in order to declare success. For each **key result**, identify a single, named individual who is accountable for achieving that result. (Although most results will require a team of implementers, saying that "everybody" is *accountable* doesn't work.) Every **strategic goal**, **key result**, and **action step** requires a single named individual who is accountable for knowing where you are, why you are there, and what you are doing about it. This use of accountability is similar to how the CFO of a company accounts for the revenue the salespeople produced and the operating expenses the production department incurred.

Each named party is accountable for maintaining **action steps** that are actually moving toward achieving the **key results**. **Action steps** are bursts of activity, each with a due date within 90 days, driven by a single named individual.

> **You must intellectually rip up last year's plan and rebuild it based on today's issues and insights.**

Putting it all together

Planning is a process rather than an event. (That's why plans are stored on computers or printed on paper rather than chiseled into stone tablets.) Once a year, set aside a couple of days with the current planning team to close out last year's plan and create this year's plan. Simply hauling out last year's plan and adding a thin new coat of shellac can't possibly address all the changes that have taken place over the course of a year. The assumptions you built into

TEAM PLANNING: THE CATALYST FOR SUCCESSFUL STRATEGY

the **strategy** last year will have been tested – some verified, others disproved. You will have identified unanticipated opportunities. Everyone on your team will have a greater understanding of the markets, products, technology, and competitive environment. The planning team – and everyone else in the market – is a year smarter and likely changed. Many of the company's **strategic goals** have been accomplished and become the status quo. Other **strategic goals** and their **key results** will require more focus to get implemented.

So, you must intellectually rip up last year's plan and rebuild it based on today's issues and insights.

You can accelerate your progress by making sure that each action you take today is consistent with where you want to be within one quarter, one year, five years, and beyond. Ask yourself: *Why* are you taking this particular action today? It's to produce a specific result that supports reaching a strategic goal that implements your **strategy**, one that is consistent with your **mission** and **vision**.

The **vision** is how the future, to which you will contribute, will be different. It gives you a stable base for decades – five, ten, or thirty years. A generation from now. Your company's core values and core purpose act as anchor and stabilizer, especially during periods of rapid change. The Big Hairy Audacious Goal inspires your team. Here's an example of how this might look for a hypothetical service company:

Values: Customer first, excellence, integrity

Purpose: Provide superior solutions in support of mission critical communications

Big Hairy Audacious Goal: Sail though $100 million

Because **vision** is stable for decades it doesn't have a lot of detail. A logical question is *how* to achieve it. The **mission** provides a stable focus for three to five years, a base from which to achieve the **vision**. It helps define what your company does and does not do. It communicates to and focuses the company around an affirmation of *what* the company wants to be, *what* customers it wants to do it for, *how* it wants to do it, and reminds everyone *why* they do it. For example:

> *To be the leading system integrator delivering mission-critical communications solutions to government agencies. Applying our expertise, resources, and technology creates a legacy and builds value for our customers, employees and owners.*

Even with just one or two paragraphs of detail, an obvious question is *how* the **mission** gets achieved. The **strategy** provides a stable focus for one and a half to three years. (The picture it paints is set five years out, but with a full page of detail in the strategic plan it evolves over a shorter time period.) **Strategy** provides the transition between the vagueness of a **vision** and **mission** and the specifics of **strategic goals** and their supporting action plans. For example, using the same hypothetical company, the **strategy** looks like this:

> *$20 million, internally grown, with consistent 15 percent EBITDA Expanded market to include federal as well and local and state government agencies. Grown to 50 percent federal.*
>
> *…*
>
> *Supporting business with under 80 employees. Developed over 10 middle managers.*
>
> *Diversified so no one customer represents more than 25 percent of our revenue.*

> **What makes a goal strategic is that it will literally change the status quo.**

How do you implement your **strategy**? How do you make real that visualization of where you want to be within three to five years? Four to six **strategic goals** change the company's status quo, putting it on the path to achieving its **strategy**. What makes a goal strategic is that it will literally change the status quo, involve multiple departments, and require a sustained commitment from the senior team. Here's how our hypothetical company's strategic goals might

TEAM PLANNING: THE CATALYST FOR SUCCESSFUL STRATEGY

look. Note that each goal has a single individual assigned to it, as discussed above in Step 3.

1. Dramatically grow sales and revenue. Pat Hayes
2. Build partnerships. Fran Diaz
3. Enhance the organization. Chuck Griffin
4. Expand our infrastructure. Raj Cox

How do you actually achieve your **strategic goals**? Achieving the set of **key results** for each **strategic goal** implements them. For example:

…

2. Build partnerships. Fran Diaz

2.1 We've identified a complete set of partners to support system integration.

Jim

2.2 We've identified the equipment manufacturers to complete our solution set. Lynn

…

How do you actually achieve a **key result**? Executing the right **action steps** in the here and now, within the next 90 days, produces the **key results**. **Action steps** are bursts of action sandwiched between the day-to-day operational chaos. Each **action step** has a single owner and a drop-dead date for completion. For example:

…

2.2 We've identified the equipment manufacturers to complete our solution set. Lynn

2.2.1 Sign reseller contracts. Lynn within 30 days

49

2.2.2 Create portfolio deck.	Dan	within 60 days
2.2.3 Train sales on products.	Dan	within 90 days
...		

Once the team decides what the company wants to accomplish, it needs to communicate it to everyone who can help make it real. Document the plan quickly, within a week of the planning meeting. Present the key aspects of the plan to the whole company. Initiate implementation immediately. (Chapter 9 discusses how to sustain implementation of your plan.)

> **When the stakes are high, it pays to get the help of a professional facilitator who can take you through a proven process.**

The CEO and executive leadership team need to create and own the plan. You always get a better result when the people implementing the plan have shaped it and believe in it. If you engage outside consultants to help with strategic planning, the best role for them is facilitating the planning process. Companies go through their planning process once a year, but professional planning facilitators execute a planning process every week. They bring a proven process and an enriched facilitation with stories, models, and questions for cross pollination that spring from extensive experience with a variety of teams in multiple situations. When the stakes are high, it pays to get the help of a professional facilitator who can take you through a proven process. Specific **key results** in the plan may require additional outside expertise. Consultants are most effective when they are targeted to deliver specific results such as research, process development, or training, etc.

    The ancient Greeks loved to gamble with dice. Despite their tradition of mathematical expertise, they gave identical odds to the pair of dice adding up to seven or twelve. Why? Because they believed that the outcome of each throw was in the hands of the gods on Mount Olympus. It never occurred to them that they had any control over the outcome. Like the ancient Greeks, many executives believe that the fate of their company is totally in the hands of others. All they think they can do is react the best they can. Strategic planning enables you to understand the odds and proactively put the future in *your* hands.

Your strategic business plan is not the end of process, it is just the beginning. As Peter Drucker reminded us, "Plans are only good intentions unless they immediately degenerate into hard work."

The chapters that follow delve into the strategic issues to consider during a planning session. Issues that directly contribute to growing value.

The next chapter deals with the good, the bad, and the ugly truth about growth. Setting direction starts with a visualization of how big you want and/or need to be. You need to not only determine *what* that answer is, you and your executive leadership team have to understand *why* and *how* you can achieve the growth. You can't assume everyone in your organization understands the strategic role of growth.

The strategic planning meeting can be held off site with the team coming together physically to share their insights and perspectives. Being together in the same location creates a "space" that enhances teamwork, innovation, and trust.

Holding the meeting virtually with video conferencing tools like Zoom can result in the same positive outcomes, albeit achieved somewhat differently.

Both meeting paradigms need to utilize methodologies that facilitate successful meetings. Physical meetings carry the overhead of having participants travel to the location, the cost of the space, catering, etc. Virtual meetings don't incur those costs but require the participants to have the technology and Internet to reliably access the meeting as well as the discipline to remain fully present while being physically in a home or office with its distractions.

It is important to use a facilitator skilled in getting the best results from whichever meeting format you choose.

CHAPTER SUMMARY

Team Planning: The Catalyst for Successful Strategy

What are the major concepts in this chapter?

- Everyone in a company has a visualization of the future that shapes how they prioritize and execute their daily actions. The more aligned and coherent those visualizations of the future are, the more they reinforce each other and create synergy. The less they are aligned, the more frustration will result.
- Strategic planning is a process not an event. The strategic planning process you use must be sustainable. This means it has to be simple enough to fit within the constraints of your available resources.
- The only way to produce a result is to finish what you start. That requires a platform that is stable long enough to initiate, complete, and reap the rewards. Each element of a strategic plan – vision, mission, strategy, and strategic goals – provides a stability of focus long enough to produce the strategic result.
- The strategic planning process that creates the strategic plan is even more important than the plan itself.
- Virtual meetings with a skilled facilitator can be as effective as in-person meetings. It might be ideal when team members are located in separate locations and time zones.

Why are these major concepts important?

- Doing the right things adequately will always produce better outcomes than doing the wrong things well.

How can you apply these major concepts?

- Follow a proven strategic planning process.

Want more? Download a FREE workbook at myrna.com/books

Chapter 4

The Good, the Bad, and the Ugly Truth About Growth

"Are you green and growing or ripe and rotting?"

Ray Kroc

"Without continual growth and progress, such words as improvement, achievement, and success have no meaning."

Benjamin Franklin

On the first day of the strategic planning retreat, the Omega Group's executive team took the pledge to "never do anything stupid because of something written on a piece of paper." Then they set about creating a shared visualization of their company's future, a key element of their strategic planning process. As their facilitator, I asked each team member how big they *wanted* the company to be within five years. I wasn't asking for a forecast or prediction, but their personal visualization, with an explanation of why they picked that number.

Before anyone could volunteer an answer, Sean, Omega's director of IT, spoke up passionately. "Growth creates nothing but problems. Why can't we just stay the size we are?" There was stunned silence for an uncomfortable period of time. I, and most of the team, assumed that every executive understood why growth is important.

I asked Sean why he felt so negative about growth. "Well, we have doubled in size over the past five years, but the only difference I see is that we seem to be working twice as hard with no obvious benefits." Getting excited, he continued: "We added all those people and machines, and when the revenue didn't immediately show up we had to tighten our belts and downsize. We ended up breaking promises to a lot of good people, and the survivors' morale really tanked."

What started as a simple question evolved into an in-depth discussion. The Omega Group's executive team dug into understanding why growth is important, as well as its good, bad, and ugly truths. In this chapter, we put the strategy for revenue and profit growth in context, exploring why size matters. Along the way we will revisit how the Omega Group answered Sean's question.

> **Chapter focus**
>
> This chapter discusses the strategic role of growth and why you need to decide how big and profitable you want and/or need to be in the future. You can't assume everyone in your organization understands the strategic role of growth.

Why size matters

The chemistry of growth starts with an agreement on *what* size the organization wants to be in five years, with size usually measured in revenue and profit. The team gets comfortable with *why* it wants to be that size, usually for reasons including some mix of countering competition, supporting new technology, reaching sustainable critical mass, or tapping the IPO market. Through its plan, the team outlines *how* it intends to achieve that size. Let's explore the good, bad, and ugly aspects of growth, pointing out the pitfalls that your company faces and the solutions best suited to help you manage growth the good way.

Owners expect their company to increase in value. When it's time to realize that value, it will be determined by:

- Future income or after tax-tax cash flows or savings discounted to their present values and adjusted for investment risks. The better positioned the company is for future performance, the higher the current value will be.
- Market value based on what buyers have paid for similar assets. The better positioned the company is in the marketplace, the higher the value.
- Cost that a prudent investor would pay for a similar asset.

Increasing long-term value requires growth. Consider how a public company's stock value is established by two factors. The first is its current operational profitability. The second is a multiplier that represents the market's expectation of future growth. The future growth constant can be calculated by dividing the current selling *price* of the stock by the current *earnings*, the so-called P/E Ratio.

- Stock Price = Annual Earnings x P/E Ratio
- The P/E Ratio can be thought of as the market's assessment of your growth potential.

Current operating profitably is a tactical challenge. Growth is a strategic challenge and the C-level executive's number one challenge.

Any discussion about a strategy for revenue and profit growth needs to be done in the context of company size. Let's look at exactly why size matters. I'm often asked, "Isn't it good enough to have a strategy to be the leader – as long as our company does the right things, who cares what size we will become?"

Suppose that you ask an architect to design a new headquarters building. The first question she will ask is "How many square feet do you need?" You can't just say, "Well, that all depends on how the market responds to our new product and what the economy looks like and …" The architect will simply ask again, "How many square feet do you need?"

Along the same lines, let's think about what can be gleaned from a simple revenue visualization like "We will hit $50 million in revenues generating a consistent 11% profit margin." There are a myriad of strategic elements that flow from a target as simple as this:

What amount of human and capital resources will be available for building and sustaining competitive advantage?

What amount of staff will need to be recruited, developed, and retained to sustain the business?

What new positions will become critical to supporting that growth – new positions like a more experienced CFO, CMO, or HR director?

What number and size of customers will be required to reach and sustain those revenue levels?

What product mix and added value will be required to support growing the profit margin to 11%?

Every member of the executive team has a future company size in mind that they consider when making their daily decisions. It's the way we're wired. Having every employee share the same number (i.e., for gross sales or total revenues) creates a form of chemical coherence where each person's individual action supports and amplifies every other person's actions.

> **You can't assume that every executive, much less every employee, understands why growth is important.**

The ugly truths about growth

One ugly truth is that you can't assume that every executive, much less every employee, understands why growth is important.

It is an ugly truth that during the early days at Omega Group, all they had to do was focus on revenue, and the profit would take care of itself. Expenses always seemed to lag revenue, with the gap filled by growing productivity. Now Omega was at a stage where profit had to be managed, the same as revenue.

There are myriad reasons why it isn't enough to focus exclusively on revenue. For one, growth is non-linear. All too often, I see companies budgeting by taking the forecast annual revenue and generating a monthly budget by dividing by twelve. However, revenue just doesn't happen that way. It doesn't grow by a fixed percentage monthly. Similarly, revenue doesn't increase evenly every year over a five-year horizon. The reality is that companies operate within a recurring, two-step cycle. Investments in business development lead to a jump in sales one, two, or three years later. The growth in revenue leads to a mix of business with uneven profitability and pressure on capacity. Rationalizing the business and increasing capacity then becomes the focus. The investments that companies make in rationalizing their business and increasing capacity serve to increase costs while creating excess capacity. In turn, this drives the company's focus back to business development.

There is a sweet spot when business exactly matches capacity, but that moment is fleeting. This is also a dangerous period for a company. The profit margins are good, leading to hubris as the company commits to fancier company cars, unsustainable benefits, and above-market compensation. As the company grows, management tends to spend more time looking internally, compared to the early days, when the CEO and her team spent time with actual customers. With growth, company executives tend to spend more and more time interacting with company employees, losing touch with the marketplace.

Growth is also subject to a natural strategic law that increases concentrations. (See Chapter 5 for more on the chemistry of concentration.) For example, one of our clients faced the challenge of 90 percent of their revenue coming from contracts issued through one government agency. Growth had been easy. All they had to do was continue to sell a product they knew how to produce to a purchasing agent who knew and appreciated them. That had been an excellent strategy with superior profitability and continuous growth – at least unless the agency had a cutback or the purchasing agent was replaced. They recognized the risk, and established a strategy that included strategic goals to diversify their customer base. Their strategy reflected the reality that net profit would be lower during the initial new market development implementation phase. It also reflected the need to adjust the sales incentive plan to maintain sufficient sales focus on developing new relationships that would likely take one to three years before generating significant new revenue. It took real discipline to sustain the focus on winning new business. (We discuss risk in more depth in Chapter 5.)

STSC Inc., a company where I spent fifteen years of my early career, recognized that sometime in the future our core market could begin to decline. Over the years we thought we were investing in multiple new market opportunities but, alas, when we drilled down we found the investment dollars were actually subsidizing inefficient operations. The beginning of the end silently occurred when STSC's salespeople were no longer successful in signing up new customers for our product several years before revenue started to decline. Growth from existing customers hid the fact that STSC's business model was no longer viable. Warren Buffet described this phenomenon best when he observed that "you don't know who's swimming naked until the tide goes out."

Another ugly truth about growth is that often you have no choice but to grow. Markets mature as competitors and customers get smarter every year. The ante required to stay in the game gets higher every year. Customers' expectations for quality, quantity, timeliness, and cost keep ratcheting up. Keeping your company competitive requires ever-increasing levels of investment. Without revenue growth, you won't have the resources to upgrade your people, products, and systems. Sometimes you have to grow or die, even if it requires making a "bet-the-company" decision. Changes in the marketplace come up and grab small to mid-size companies by the collar and shake them out of their "maintain the status quo" mode. Changes also create executive angst, which team planning can address.

The good about growth

So with all these ugly challenges, why would you want to grow your company? Benjamin Franklin had a terrific answer: "Without continual growth and progress, such words as improvement, achievement, and success have no meaning."

Going back to our initial example at Omega Group, Sean's fellow executives found it easy to enumerate the reasons in favor of growth. The operations manager pointed out, "We can't afford to invest in process improvement until we have sufficient volume to justify it. More revenue, and the profit it generates, provides the resources to acquire more modern and productive machinery. Without growth, how else could we have afforded the new ERP system and your staff expansion, Sean?"

The HR director noted that the first question every potential hire asks is "are you growing?" Growth creates new opportunities for advancement and potential for annual increases in compensation. A steady stream of new employees sustains a healthy diversity. The HR director pointed out that without new employees, the average age of employees gets a year older every 12 months, and eventually between attrition and retirement, the entire workforce will be gone. A growing company provides career paths and attracts the best talent.

The Omega CFO reminded the team that banks don't want to lend to stagnant companies. They want to lend to well-managed, growing companies. The sales manager noted that prospective customers preferred to work with vendors they believed would have the resources to support them in the future. "The cost of sales is lower when we have strong word of mouth and testimonials from existing customers. We are now seen by our top two customers as partners. They even invite us to *their* planning meetings."

The purchasing manager added: "Don't forget the leverage we get with volume purchases from our vendors. When we are a major, growing customer, we get priority treatment when there are shortages." The head of R&D recalled that "our last product launch went a lot faster because we had lots of ready-made alpha and beta customers to help us quickly work the bugs out."

Paul, the Omega Group CEO, said, "It's all about our ability to manage risk. With a stable customer base and recurring revenue, we can manage riskier investments." The nature of the risk he mentioned was how long it would take to reach break-even with a new product, office, or market. "Usually the opportunities with the greatest potential," Paul continued, "pose a greater risk. You, know – the Risk/Reward Trade Off." Paul also highlighted the competitive advantages of gaining and retaining market share leadership.

"Our competitors are finding it harder to afford to keep up with us. As long as we manage the company well, our superior productivity and profit margins will make us the best bet for our customers."

As the planning meeting's facilitator, I pointed out that their growth, and the systems and processes it funded, enabled them to remain profitable during economic downturns and market shifts. I also reiterated the power of the "Experience Curve." The more units you produce, the better you get at it. In Malcolm Gladwell's book *Outliers*, he shared research that suggests it isn't enough to have exceptional talent. It also takes 10,000 hours of experience to become a true expert at anything. Customers migrate to vendors they see as experts.

> **Corporate culture manifests itself in how employees prioritize their daily tasks.**

What's bad about growth?

There are surprising limits to growth and performance. Growth changes everything, and if you embrace it, change isn't automatically bad. However, as with all change, growth creates short-term winners and losers. For example, the skill sets of employees need to change along with the company. Sometimes this requires the replacement of hardworking, loyal employees. If it is unlikely that a bookkeeper can be trained as a CFO, the loyal bookkeeper will likely have to be replaced, becoming one of the "losers." I've seen many CEOs hesitate to act because of the personal promises they made years ago to attract these very people.

Corporate culture manifests itself in how employees prioritize their daily tasks. As a company grows, the things that are most important will change. For example, a small manufacturer can cherry-pick customers and prioritize large orders over small ones. Operators who "know" that they have to prioritize large orders from existing customers will impede a company's ability to attract and support emerging (i.e., initially smaller) prospects in the market. Further, large customers are generally not interested in new technologies unless they optimize the features and costs of the existing components they are utilizing in their products. This phenomenon has been dubbed "the innovator's dilemma.[4]" For example, PC manufacturers weren't interested in using physically smaller disk drives. They pushed their disk drive vendors to make the drives have more capacity, operate faster, and cost less while remaining the same physical size. Physically smaller drives that enabled new products like laptops didn't get commercially developed by existing disk drive companies; they came from startups without an existing customer base they had to cater to.

Most founders enjoy applying their operational skills to growing the company in the early years. With growth, the CEO's focus needs to move from being the chief salesman or product developer to concentrating on the three non-delectable CEO tasks:

- building the management team,
- making the "bet-the-company" decisions, and,
- championing the strategic planning process.

We once had to drive this home with a client's CEO who insisted on reviewing each and every vendor payment. While that was a reasonable use of a few minutes of his time when there were only dozens of checks a week, it made no sense when it consumed hours of his time to review hundreds of checks, many of them less than half a percent of the company's monthly budget.

With growth, the risks a company faces will change. When a company is growing rapidly, office space, branch offices, and new computer systems come in ever-bigger dollar chunks and multi-year commitments. Cutting back incurs a larger short-term financial impact. (There are the greater costs from severance pay, order cancellation fees, and monthly lease and rental payments for unused machines and office space.) When you're making decisions like this, ask yourself, "What's the worst that could happen?" As you grow, the "worst" gets larger and requires more consideration before committing resources.

Growth leaves a wake of legacy customers, products, and employees. The old saying that "you need to dance with the one who brung you" is a formula for failure. As you grow, you'll find there are customers that are no longer large enough to warrant the company resources they consume. There are products that aren't strategic enough to attract the corporate resources

---

4   Clayton M. Christensen. *The Innovator's Dilemma: When New Technologies Cause Great Firms to Fail.* (Harvard Business Review Press, 2013)

to keep them competitive. There are employees flailing in a job that now requires skills and competence they don't have. Healthy companies review their employee, customer, and product bases regularly and take proactive action to transition the ones that no longer fit their size and strategy. They move them to other companies that can better serve them. This process of "rationalizing" maintains profit margins by phasing out products that have become unprofitable, improves customer service by focusing on customers with the greatest growth potential, and improves morale and performance by maintaining a productive match between each employee and their job position.

When you are a start-up operating from a garage, customers have modest expectations and tend to be understanding and supportive. They say things like "It's amazing how good they are given their size." Employees accept minimal compensation and good investors are patient. However, once you've "made it," everyone's expectations jump, often to unsustainable levels.

A secret about growth

The greatest limit to a company's growth is the belief of its executive team. If the team is convinced it can't grow faster, it won't commit to implementing the strategic things that enable that growth. I had the opportunity to work with Larry Ellison, founder of Oracle, in the company's early years. Oracle doubled in size every year for thirteen years in a row. In the same time period other companies stumbled when they experienced relatively modest growth rates of 25 percent. What was Oracle's secret?

The secret was growing their *ability to remain in control* faster than they grew their revenue. Oracle established a strategy for high-growth, aggressively investing in improving their people's competence, their processes, their forecasting ability, and their control systems.

No company grows by cutting expenses or being overly cautious. Companies grow by improving their productivity, business acumen, and overall ability to manage risk. Remember that the opportunities with the highest potential return usually demand the capability to manage a higher level of risk. This is known as the Risk/Return Tradeoff. The most common risk is that an investment will take longer than expected to pay off. (Often, it takes much longer.) Companies lose their investment capital when they open new offices or develop major new products without the capacity to quickly make adjustments and sustain them until they start paying off. (I talk in more detail about strategic risks in Chapter 5.)

In summary, the shared visualization of *what* size the company wants to be in the future sets the frame for the entire strategy. Understanding *why* that revenue and profit number was set motivates everyone to adjust their daily priorities to support it. The rest of the strategy answers *how* that size will be achieved.

Remember that value often means more than merely financial for different stakeholders. For example, they may find value in advancement, being green, quality, respect, stability, etc.

In the next chapter, we explore the various forms of risk and why managing them is a key component of any company's strategy. A key success factor for companies is how well they can manage risk. The greater their capability, the more confident they can be when investing in growth opportunities that require greater risk management. When it comes to managing risk, there is no excuse for the leadership team to be blindsided.

CHAPTER SUMMARY

The Good, the Bad, and the Ugly Truth About Growth

What are the major concepts in this chapter?

- You can't assume everyone in your organization understands the strategic role of growth.
- You have to decide how big and profitable you want to be in the future.
- You have to determine how big and profitable you need to be in the future.

Why are these major concepts important?

- Everyone in the company consciously or unconsciously shapes and prioritizes their daily decisions based on their belief about expected growth.
- Increasing long-term value requires growth. Like a public stock, company value is established by two factors – current operational profitability multiplied by the expectation of future growth. (Stock Price = Annual Earnings x P/E Ratio, where P/E Ratio is the market's assessment of your growth potential.)
- Size establishes the landscape where you will be working in the future.
- There are external forces that require you to grow. Customer expectations grow yearly and their vendors need to keep pace if you want to continue serving them.
- Uncontrolled growth will lead to disasters such as running out of capacity, capital, and competency.

How can you apply these major concepts?

- Establish a five-year revenue number that everyone agrees to, sufficient to meet internal and external demands, and that could be achievable with the strategy. For example, "Within five years we will support $35 million in sales, 70 percent from organic growth, 30 percent from new markets internally developed or acquired."

- Establish an agreed-upon profit number. For example, "Within five years our improved product mix and increased value-added will deliver a consistent pre-tax profit of at least 13.5 percent."

- Establish an understanding that you are communicating a plan, not providing a license to do something stupid. Invoke the pledge to "never do something stupid because of something written on a piece of paper."

- Establish expectations for growing the infrastructure in support of growth. For example, "We will be operating from six regional offices, up from today's three, and an expanded headquarters. We will increase total headcount to 256 full-time equivalent employees, increasing productivity to $310,000 per employee from today's $250,000."

- Establish expectations for non-financial values.

- Establish systems that enhance your ability to anticipate and act on problems before they become a crisis. For example, "We will fully deploy an ERP system."

Want more? Download a FREE workbook at myrna.com/books

Like this book? Please leave a review at Amazon.com!

Chapter 5
Market, Technical, and Financial Risk

"A ship in port is safe, but that's not what ships are built for."

Rear Admiral Grace Murray Hopper

"It seems to be a law of nature, inflexible and inexorable, that those who will not risk cannot win."

John Paul Jones

When does bad news reveal good decisions? At the start of the sixth annual strategic planning meeting I facilitated by Acme Manufacturing, Greg, the CEO, shared some bad news with his senior executive team. "Well, it finally happened – Groot just filed for bankruptcy. We will have to tighten our belts and cover the loss of Groot's business."

"It's more than that, I'm afraid," said Faran, the CFO. "We will have to write off more than two months of receivables."

Fred, the relatively new director of operations, chimed in: "I hate to pour gas on the fire, but we also have a sizable inventory of custom parts and raw materials that we will have to eat. What percentage of our business was Groot?"

"Twenty percent!" the chorus of longer-tenured executives replied.

"But it was over 80 percent five years ago," said Greg. "Thank God we recognized the risk of that concentration then and forced ourselves to diversify our customer base in case this day ever came."

Before moving on, Faran couldn't resist speaking up. "And that, Fred, is why we continue to ask you to find production time for testing our new product line instead of running more of our most popular product. We need to continue to diversify to keep our largest concentration of business under 25 percent."

> **Chapter focus**
>
> This chapter discusses the multiple sources of strategic risk and offers strategies for managing them. It reviews commonly recognized risks such as over-concentration in one source of business, natural disasters and the sudden arrival of major competition. It highlights the less commonly recognized risks of wasting your investment dollars, insufficient focus to fully realize the benefits of the Experience Curve, and being overcome by newer, better solutions to the problems your products solve.

Managing risk

Do you know how to recognize a risk like the one Acme faced when you see it? Managing risk is a major element of the chemistry of growth. You must understand strategic risks – what they are, how to identify them, and how to assess and manage them from a strategic perspective. Financial risk is embedded in all these risks, since the impact of all risks is ultimately financial. If Acme Manufacturing had unexpectedly suddenly lost 80 percent of their revenue, it would have bankrupted them within weeks. Every strategic risk ultimately translates into an operational financial risk.

> **The greater a company's ability to manage risk, the greater its ability to act on high risk/reward opportunities.**

Nitroglycerin is a powerful explosive, and extremely sensitive to physical shock. It degrades over time to even more unstable forms. Aware in the 1860s that nitroglycerin was more powerful than black powder, the leaders of the Central Pacific Railroad Company realized its use could speed up the construction of the Transcontinental Railroad's Summit Tunnel by as much as 74 percent if the company could manage the risk. They reduced the risk to acceptable levels by producing the nitroglycerin on site, eliminating the periodic explosions suffered when shipping it. They further reduced the risk through use of Chinese workers who were especially skilled in safely using the volatile substance. Developing the acumen to manage the higher risk, they were able to realize the greater return. However, nitroglycerin remained a volatile, risky chemical.

Alfred Nobel studied the properties of nitroglycerin and developed a way to make it much safer to handle, in the form of dynamite. This approach to risk management was a more valuable strategy, one that made him rich beyond the dreams of avarice.

Analogously, managing risk in a company can be done in different ways. One can reduce the chance of shipping bad products, for example, through 100 percent inspection. Re-engineering the manufacturing process to eliminate the volatility that produces bad products to begin with is a more valuable way to manage the risk.

One of the major quality measures of a company and its senior management team is its capability for managing risk. Every strategic decision contains a mix of risk and reward. The greater a company's ability to manage risk, the greater its ability to act on high risk/reward opportunities. Strategies to improve your executive team's ability to manage risk will pay great dividends, especially in turbulent times. Enhanced reporting and tracking systems provide strategic and operational warnings early enough to allow modest corrective action before a small risk matures into a crisis. Continuous investment in developing the acumen of the executive team leads to smarter decisions.

Six sources of strategic risk

There are six major sources of strategic risks. Two that have the potential to wipe a company out overnight are:

Unhealthy concentrations that make a company vulnerable to the loss of a business keystone – a major customer, a uniquely skilled employee, a custom machine, a single raw material supplier, etc.

Unpredictable, high-impact events such as a natural disaster, facility fire, economic crash, etc.

There are also four risks that, while they are unlikely to wipe out your company overnight, could smother it over the next three to five years:

Superior competitive solutions to the problem your company's current products address. This could be through replacement technology, integration with another solution, or problem prevention/elimination. Sometimes the replacement can be technically inferior but with a superior cost structure that attracts sufficient customers to allow your competitors to keep growing and improving.

Insufficient development investments of attention, time, and resources to realize a usable return. An example would be investments that don't end up creating future products and/or markets.

Insufficient volume and focus to generate sufficient continuous improvement of products, sales and operations to sustain profitability and competitiveness.

A CEO that believes they know it all and takes extreme action without the benefit of the insights and perceptions of their leadership team or CEO peer group. Insular management or insular philosophy can be fatal.

Unhealthy concentrations

Managing risk requires the balancing of competing demands on resources. Operational needs are immediate and can easily drive an unhealthy balance, with the most obvious risk to revenue coming from an unmanageable concentration such as customers, product, or market.

Returning to our example at the start of this chapter, Acme Manufacturing needed to grow volume fast to generate sufficient work to cover the cost of its expensive presses and operators. A few years earlier, Groot had started purchasing custom parts from Acme. Groot, a fast-growing leader in its niche market, quickly accounted for over 80 percent of Acme's revenue. It was a sweet business model, selling a product Acme knew how to build to a customer who knew and trusted them. The risk of basing the business on just one major client became real years later when Groot filed for bankruptcy. However, there were also very real risks had Acme prematurely diversified its customer base beyond Groot:

- Developing new customers and products prematurely would sap resources with the uncertain promise of future sales. There would be less profit and cash flow to meet Acme's own day-to-day operational needs. There would be the constant need to shortchange developmental investment in order to meet short-term operational needs. When a company consistently shortchanges development, it might as well flush those investment dollars down the drain.

- With Acme's attention and resources spread thin, Groot's needs wouldn't get the timely response they required. Neglect could motivate them to find a new vendor more committed to them. Once Groot started on that path, they would begin to review and question everything about the relationship with Acme, including (and especially) pricing, further depressing profit and cash flow.

- Moving resources away from building Groot's volume would slow Acme's movement along the Experience Curve, hindering their achievement of both critical mass and a competitive advantage. (More about these topics in Chapter 8.)

Acme's decision to accept the short-term risk and focus resources on building their business around Groot was rational and the best way to achieve critical mass. However, even after they had achieved critical mass, Groot had become such a part of the status quo that no one thought about the growing risk of having so much depend on one customer.

Seven years earlier, Acme's executive team had identified the loss of Groot's business as the biggest potential threat to their business. "That won't happen," Greg, the Acme Manufacturing CEO, had said at the time. "I'm out to their plant monthly. I'm on the phone with Groot's purchasing agent weekly. We have excellent quality, perfect on-time delivery, and with the experience their volume has provided, I can't see how anyone can match, much less undercut our price. They will never leave us."

During that strategic planning meeting seven years before, I asked the Acme team, "What if Groot gets acquired by a company with its own manufacturing supply chain? Or, what if they go bankrupt? There are more ways to lose a customer than poor performance on Acme's part."

What was the outcome of that year's strategic planning session? It was to establish a risk component in Acme Manufacturing's strategy to keep the largest concentration of business under 25 percent. **Why** 25 percent? Because the executive team felt that any sudden loss of revenue above that percentage would likely be unrecoverable. (The team did a simple "what if" exercise to determine how they could cut monthly expenses enough to keep the doors open if they had to.) *How* was that strategy implemented?

- Acme became more watchful with regards to maintaining accounts receivables. They became more conservative about purchasing equipment and hiring full-time employees to meet growing demand from Groot. Outsourcing work at peak periods reduced margins, but wouldn't leave Acme with potentially unusable capacity should something happen to that particular customer. Simultaneously, they made sure that they never took Groot's business for granted. They assigned dedicated staff members who were personally accountable for making sure Groot was happy.
- Acme gradually shifted their priorities and resources to building up a new revenue base. Since Groot was the major player in their niche

MARKET, TECHNICAL AND FINANCIAL RISK

market, this required identifying an expansion market. After two and a half years invested in exploring three likely prospects, Acme established an initial customer base in a new market with attractive potential. The new market was large and growing, appreciated vendors like Acme that could apply manufacturing expertise to solving their problems, and was full of prospective customers willing to give new players like Acme a shot at their business.

- Acme made sure that everyone in the company understood the importance of fully supporting orders from customers in the new market. Their new customers started by placing small trial orders with Acme for difficult parts that their existing vendors weren't interested in making. It would have been easy for Acme's sales and operations teams to view difficult parts, low volume, and small to negative margins as a waste of time. Without constant reinforcement of why these small "unprofitable" orders were important, well-meaning employees could have sabotaged the new strategy with late deliveries and bad quality.

Less obvious concentrations

Concentration risk can show up in less obvious ways. Consider, for example, Friend Finance, a small-business financing company that was built on the personal relationship between its founder Taylor and its major clients. Each client felt that they weren't buying services from a company; they were contracting with Taylor as an individual. As a result, she couldn't realize the equity in the business, because without her day-to-day involvement, there was no business. Further, the business had limited growth potential since she had to be involved personally with every client. We asked her whether she was building a business or a making a living. "Building a business" was her answer, so she and the company established a strategic goal to reduce dependence on her to under 20 percent of revenue within five years. Six years later, Taylor realized the equity she had built by selling out to another company, and retired. Her management team stayed on as the new, combined company was positioned for rapid national expansion. This positioning had been part of their strategy, and being acquired provided the resources for the management team to implement that strategy.

Concentrations are a naturally occurring phenomenon. For example, when you make "cowboy coffee," you drop ground coffee mixed with eggshells in a pot of boiling water. Initially, the ground coffee and eggshells are evenly distributed in the water. As the coffee brews, a single coffee ground attaches itself to an eggshell. That eggshell then becomes more "attractive" to other coffee grounds. Each time a coffee ground attaches itself to an existing clump, it makes that clump even more attractive to the remaining coffee grounds. This is a chemical process known as flocculation. Eventually, the clumps become so heavy they fall to the bottom of the pot, allowing you to enjoy a reasonably grounds-free cup of coffee.

Another example is the Internet, which was designed to be a robust network with so many potential paths from any point on the network to any other point that a nuclear attack wouldn't knock it out. Yet today connectivity depends on about five percent of the hubs. Why? A hub with the largest number of connections is the most logical hub for a new connection. Once you have added the new connection, the hub becomes even more attractive for the next connection. Before very long, a network where every hub had an equal number of connections morphs into a network where 4 percent of the hubs carry over 64 percent of the traffic.

Consider how concentrations happen in a business over time. You build a customer base of people who know and trust you. You build the operational capability to provide certain products reliably and on time. Your salespeople have a monthly sales quota to fill. The logical way to meet that quota is to prioritize selling what your salespeople know you can build to people and markets who already know the company, i.e., selling more product to existing customers in existing markets. Over time, each salesperson focuses on selling to the customer who is already buying the most from them, increasing the percentage of business that flows through that single client. Before you know it, you have a risky concentration. The risky concentration could be with a single customer, a single part, a single market, or a single salesperson. You can ask the sales team to pursue new customers or sell new products, but such requests will end up uncompleted, at the bottom of their to-do list, unless you have a well-communicated strategic focus on diversifying.

Unpredictable, high-impact events

Superior Tubing's Arkansas plant was destroyed by a tornado. Luckily, the employees were able to get to safety before the tornado hit. Summing up the company's reaction a year and a half later, the CEO reiterated the good news. "Our Arkansas plant has not only returned to full production, the company's two other plants set new production records. Even better, the marketplace is recognizing how well we managed the catastrophe."

Superior Tubing's secret to recovery? They had identified the tornado risk years earlier and incorporated a disaster recovery program as part of their strategy. They had standardized computer systems across all three plants, making it easy to transfer the working files from the destroyed plant's backup tapes. They had put plants in multiple locations to reduce the risk of losing one. They maintained sufficient financial reserves – a mix of cash, business interruption insurance, and borrowing capacity – to tide them over. Because their employees were already cross-trained to operate a variety of different presses, they were able to quickly redeploy staff, including temporarily relocating Arkansas workers, to expand shifts at the other two undamaged plants.

Superior Tubing's disaster recovery program wasn't a dust-covered plan created so they could check "yes" on a form from their bank or government regulators. The planning team had felt it was strategically important to integrate recovery into how the company ran, rather than create a plan to recover post-disaster. For example, they regularly manufactured Plant One parts in Plant Two to handle overflow demand. When doing maintenance on Plant Two's computer system, they ran Plant Two MRP software remotely on Plant Three's computers. They didn't wait for an actual disaster to verify that a disaster recovery *plan* worked. They made their company more robust through an integrated disaster recovery *program*.

Superior competitive solutions

Best Systems knew it would just be a matter of time before their market would evaporate. They had a nice business manufacturing and supplying products based on a computer interface first introduced in military systems over fifty years ago. Their business had grown, based on products that enable military users of legacy systems to build replacement applications that communicate with existing ships and planes still using this ancient interface. In the short term, Best Systems' customers are perfectly happy to see them continue to develop new and improved versions of their products. However, the military has been executing a long-standing strategy to phase out this interface, albeit over decades. Best Systems follows a dual product/market strategy. For their legacy market, the basis of their business today, the company did the following:

- They didn't waste resources trying to sell products that would require their customer to adopt an old technology. (Doubling sales commissions isn't going to increase demand for an out-of-date technology.)
- They focused product development investments on opportunities with an 18-month ROI and/or features that enable legacy customers to defer their transition to new technology.
- They made every effort to identify and sell 100 percent of legacy technology users.
- They made every effort to motivate competitors to drop out of the market.

Best Systems' five-year strategy identified the need to identify, develop, and grow a new business to over 20 percent of total revenue. Why 20 percent and why five years? There is a strategic law that marketing professionals call the Product Life Cycle. New market or product sales don't reach their potential overnight. It takes time to build a customer base and volume. In the graph below, for example, it would take this product over four years to reach 25 percent of its annual potential. If managing risk depends on sales from a new market/product to replace an expected decline, you need to start building that new business, years ahead of time. (We explore diversification and product/market strategies in Chapter 6.)

MARKET, TECHNICAL AND FINANCIAL RISK

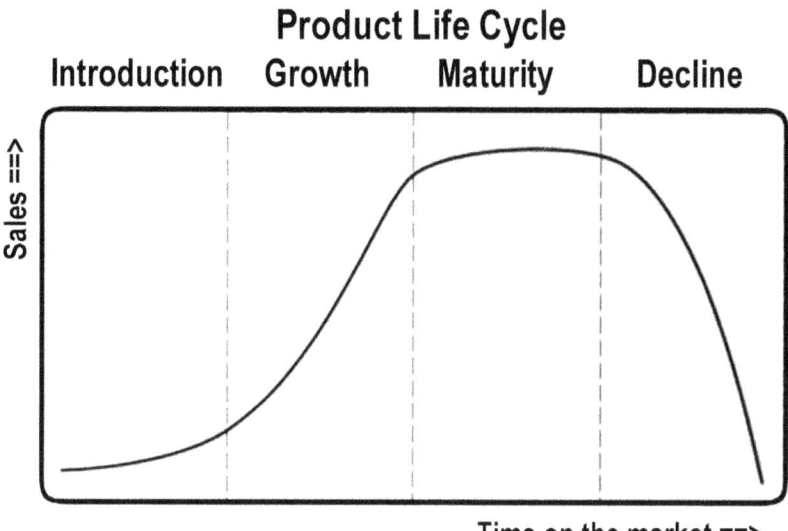

For Best Systems, the smart strategy was to identify and enter the "growth" stage of the new business before their core business entered its "decline" stage. They maintained an open mind about how to obtain that new business. If they could identify and grow it organically, all the better. Alternatively, if there was an opportunity to acquire a business, they were strategically prepared to do so.

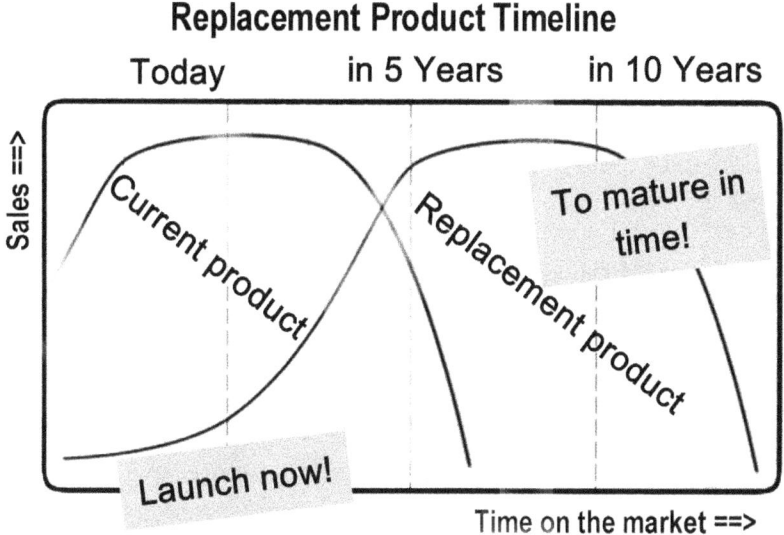

Insufficient development investments

Fun Foods' business was built on supplying a single product to movie theaters. They sold replacements when their product wore out and made sales to new theaters. Revenue plummeted when hard times hit. There weren't any new theaters being built and existing theaters deferred replacing old products. Over the years, the company had discussed developing additional products that would appeal to their theater customers. They had also discussed searching for new markets for their product. Yet, when sales plummeted they didn't have any new products or markets to fall back on. Why? In retrospect, we could see that Fun Foods had never really invested sufficiently in developing them. It had impatiently dabbled in many different areas. When they didn't see immediate results, they weren't willing to take the next step.

Luckily, Fun Foods was saved by their aggressive acquisition strategy. After a protracted, painful period of downsizing, they were able acquire a new business which, after integration and growth, enabled them to survive the decline of their core market.

A company's strategy is a mix of exploration and exploitation. President Thomas Jefferson commissioned the Lewis and Clark expedition with a clear yet broad objective, Congressional approval, funding, dedicated staff, and sufficient time to identify potential opportunities in the territory encompassed by the Louisiana Purchase. Their expedition, which lasted 28 months, is a good model for successful exploration. Once exploration has identified major opportunities, successful strategies shift to the exploitation stage. At least once a year, review your company strategy and verify the balance between exploration and exploitation.

Insufficient volume and focus

SWT Services was a small company that provided three services: staffing, web design, and technical writing. None of their customers purchased more than one service. In effect, SWT Services was three tiny companies under one corporate name. When SWT started the staffing service, they were the only firm specializing in placing technical writers. Once leaders in that niche, they now consistently lost opportunities to a local firm that only provided staffing services. By now, their competitor had more assignments in a month than SWT had in a year. Every time their competitor filled a position, they increased their file of potential hires. Every time their competitor satisfied a company's staffing need, they made it more likely they would be called the next time rather than SWT. Given their low volume, SWT Services started losing money on the staffing service. A small company can't afford to split its focus. It's challenging enough to generate a competitive volume within a single niche, not to mention three.

Every year, your company, your competition, and your industry have the opportunity to get smarter from an additional twelve months of experience. That means your company strategy must include a roadmap of how you will become more competitive. Each time you move along the Experience Curve, you should expect to figure out how to spend less to sell and deliver your product. The first time you do anything is the most expensive (in terms of time, effort, money, revision, etc.). The more times you do something, the less resources it requires. This allows you to produce more results for the same amount of resource. This forms a virtuous cycle – the more widgets you produce, the cheaper it is to produce the next widget. The cheaper the next widget, the more competitive you become. But, all of this assumes that your company follows a strategy of continuous improvement. (We dig deeper into strategies for productivity and continuous learning in Chapter 8.)

In the next chapter, we delve into why a product/market focus is essential in order to accelerate the experience curve, achieve critical mass, and sustain it. The best tool for beating the competition is a focused strategy.

A CEO that believes they know it all

Business is complex and it isn't possible to literally know it all. The most successful CEOs have developed a leadership team with insights and perspectives representing ground truths, the wisdom gained from boots on the ground. In addition, the top CEOs belong to a CEO peer group like Vistage enabling them to benefit from the insights and perspectives of a diverse mix of CEOs. (D&B analysis showed Vistage CEOs grew their companies over twice as fast as non-Vistage companies.)

CHAPTER SUMMARY

How to Identify and Manage Market, Technical, and Financial Risk

What are the major concepts in this chapter?

- Insufficient investments of attention, time, and resources to realize a usable return can kill your company's future. An example would be investments that don't end up creating future products and/or markets.
- Insufficient volume and focus to generate sufficient continuous improvement of products, sales, and operations can prevent you from sustaining profitability and competitiveness.
- Superior competitive solutions to the problems your company's current products address can be anticipated. These solutions can be implemented through replacement technology, integration with another solution, problem prevention/elimination, etc.
- Unhealthy concentrations can make a company vulnerable to the loss of a business keystone – a major customer, a uniquely skilled employee, a custom machine, a single raw material supplier, etc.
- Unpredictable, high-impact events such as terrorism, sabotage, a natural disaster, facility fire, or economic crash can hit at any time.

Why are these major concepts important?

- Not changing the status quo to reduce or eliminate the impact of these strategic risks makes the company more vulnerable to external events outside its control.
- Unmanaged strategic risks ultimately lead to major, too often fatal financial risk.
- The greater the risk you can effectively manage, the greater the potential long-term value you can create.

MARKET, TECHNICAL AND FINANCIAL RISK

How can you apply these major concepts?

- Establish a disaster recovery program that integrates the ability to recover with day-to-day operations. For example, "We will operate with at least two people cross-trained and certified to perform every critical function."

- Establish a product market strategy that accelerates moving along the Experience Curve, achieves and sustains critical mass, and increases competitive advantage. For example, "We will have significant business from at least eight of the top ten financial institutions."

- Establish a system that identifies potential new product technologies and solutions. For example, "We will never allow ourselves to be surprised by a new technology or solution."

- Establish an appropriate balance between exploration and exploitation. For example, "We will follow a disciplined development process that leads to at least 30 percent of business five years from now coming from products and/or markets we don't have today."

- Establish an upper limit for business concentrations by customer, technology, market. For example, "No single customer or product will be greater than 20 percent of revenue."

- Establish measurable goals for productivity. For example, "We will reduce the cost of providing existing products by at least 5 percent annually."

Want more? Download a FREE workbook at myrna.com/books

Like this book? Please leave a review at Amazon.com!

Chapter 6
The Chemistry of Product/Market Strategies

"Concentration is the secret of strengths in politics, in war, in trade, in short in all management of human affairs."

Ralph Waldo Emerson

"One swallow does not a summer make."

Aristotle

I vividly remember an IBM product user's group meeting. IBM, the Goliath in our market to my company's David, had the floor for a question-and-answer session. One of IBM's customers asked why they hadn't addressed a specific problem in a product we directly competed with. "You have to understand," said the IBM spokesman, "we have limited resources and can't address everything."

I smiled because my company, with a fraction of IBM's resources, was providing a complete solution to that very problem. The overall size of Goliath IBM wasn't important. What mattered was the amount of resources they were devoting to servicing customers within our market niche. As long as we were devoting more productive hours to understanding and developing solutions within our market focus than IBM, we had the competitive advantage. Every time we serviced a customer, we gained a greater insight into our niche market's needs while reducing our cost of providing the service. IBM couldn't keep up with us within our niche because their vast resources were spread across a myriad of niches. Further, we earned a reputation as the "go-to" company for products within our focused market. Every new customer became a raving fan, making it easier to sign up the next new customer.

I had an answer to the question I asked the company's founder when I joined them in 1969. "How can a little company like us compete with IBM?" The answer was by using a focused product/market strategy.

> **Chapter focus**
>
> This chapter discusses the importance of sustaining a marketplace focus that is sufficient to generate enough experience to sustain being the best at what you do while balancing the need to avoid risky concentrations. It discusses the need for a balance between exploitation of your current product/market position and exploration to develop potential future sources of revenue. It also touches on the role of M&A and partnerships, and what your profit strategy is.

Focus, focus, focus

In the chemistry of growth, no strategic laws have as great an impact as the Experience Curve and the law of Critical Mass. These laws underpin your product/market strategy. A product/market *focus* is essential in order to accelerate your progress along the experience curve, achieve critical mass in a niche or a market, and sustain it.

THE CHEMISTRY OF PRODUCT/MARKET STRATEGIES

There are many product/market strategic questions your product/market strategy answers. How exactly does your organization define the words "product" and "market"? What role should market and product diversity play in your strategy? Does your pricing hide your company's true value to customers? When should you develop new markets and when should you double down and exploit existing markets? What is your strategy for branding? How important is critical mass in your market? What's your geographic scope? What is the process for product/market expansion? It all starts with an understanding of the importance of the Experience Curve.

The Experience Curve

I can walk into a company and tell the CEO I know exactly what their problem is: *focus* and *communication*. Why? Because these are the challenges every organization faces. The strategic laws surrounding focus are at the heart of the Chemistry of Growth. Research by Boston Consulting Group in the 1960s and 1970s observed that for various industries, every time you doubled your experience, your productivity increased between 10 and 25 percent.[5] This effect has been labeled the Experience Curve, also known as the learning curve.

The chemistry of a winning product/market strategy is to define a focus that enables you to leverage the Experience Curve better than your competition. The most productive market strategy is one of exploitation – creating a virtuous cycle of adding more customers, more transactions, and more value per transaction. This should be your primary strategic focus as long as your market niche has sufficient profitable growth potential and is stable over the foreseeable future. Double down again and again, to move along the Experience Curve faster than your competitors.

Stability

Such a focus on exploitation assumes that your market is stable. Review the stability of your market as part of your annual strategic planning process.

---

5   Hax, Arnoldo C.; Majluf, Nicolas S. (October 1982), "Competitive cost dynamics: the experience curve," *Interfaces* 12 (5): 50–61, doi:10.1287/inte.12.5.50

Are there new processes or products entering the marketplace that could reduce or eliminate the value of your products? For example, what effect will 3D printers – additive manufacturing – that can create replacement parts on demand have on the value of your warehouse of spare parts? Are there any potential issues related to the raw materials used in your products? Your product line could be banned from the marketplace by new regulations limiting the use of a carcinogenic raw material, for example. Is there a looming low-cost provider that could undercut your product's price? The availability of a cheaper, imported product could overwhelm your product's market presence. What do you do if your team recognizes vulnerabilities in your market niche? It may be time to start discussing diversification.

Diversification

There are unproductive ways to think about diversification, as when government contractors daydream about entering the "stable" commercial marketplace, and commercial firms look longingly at the "lucrative" government marketplace. The reality is that whether you're heavily dependent on government contracts for your revenue or you're out playing in the commercial markets, the grass isn't really greener on the other side; there are no "safe" market niches where vulnerability never becomes an issue.

Jake was new to the strategic planning team at his specialty manufacturing company. "The automotive business goes through business cycles," he said. "We need to build a business in another market that doesn't."

"I can understand why you feel that way," replied Petra, the sales vice president. "The fact is, we are well-diversified within the automotive business because we provide cost-competitive latches to all the major players, on multiple automotive platforms. During economic downturns it's our competitors that are the minor suppliers losing business, not us. Why would we want to become a minor supplier in a different market and be the ones dropped when that market has an economic downturn?" Petra explained that the company found, much to its dismay, that each of the non-automotive markets they had played with in the past experienced downturns at the same time as the automotive market. It is very rare to find truly counter-cyclical markets. Petra noted: "Our best strategy is to exploit our presence in the automotive market and structure our company to manage the ebb and flow of that market."

I've found that seeking a safe market is not a useful reason for considering diversification into a new market. You should first look to diversify within your existing market by broadening the customer and product base. Only after you've exhausted those opportunities should you look to diversify into entirely new markets.

How to best diversify into a new market

It's best to seek out a customer from outside your current market who has already asked you to customize your product to better meet their needs. Then verify that there are enough similar prospects in that new market to build a focus around. You already have a leg up on the market research, since at least one member of the new market is utilizing your product. An alternative approach is to find an existing customer interested in developing a solution that would appeal to your other customers and potentially a new market.

Once you have a candidate, evaluate the market's potential using these four key criteria:

Is it real? Consider the classic example of imagining if only 1 percent of the Chinese market purchased your widgets!

Can we do it? Just because you have the technical capability doesn't mean your organization can actually deliver and support the proposed new market. For example, companies with low-volume, high-value, high-service products don't have the low-cost overhead structure to handle high-volume, low-price products.

Can we win? Everything is a competition. You are competing with existing players in the new market and even more significantly, competing with other company priorities.

Is it worth it? It is easy to get swept up in the romance of a new venture without taking the time to quantify what winning will be worth to you.

If you and your team can honestly answer "yes" to the four questions above, then set a strategy to establish a presence in that new market.

The Expansion Matrix™ shows this diversification strategy graphically. The best expansion strategy allows you to keep one foot anchored in a current strength, market or product, and to swing the other foot into new territory. This might mean selling something new to someone who already knows and loves you, or it might be selling something that every customer in your current market loves to a prospect in a new market. The riskiest approach is selling something you have never built before to someone who has never heard your name before. (This is also known as a startup, and it's notoriously hard to do this within an existing company.)

Expansion Matrix™

	Product 1	Product 2	New Product	New Product
Market 1	●	●	→→	→
Market 2	●	↓↓	→	→
New Market	↓↓	↓	↓	↓
New Market	↓	↓	↓	↓

Expand by developing new products for existing markets (→)
and/or moving existing products into new markets (↓)
Avoid trying to introduce new products to new markets.

Critical mass

You need multiple customers and multiple transactions before you have enough experience to earn the right to say you're "in a market." Entering a market starts as an investment. It usually costs more to obtain and service your initial transactions than you can charge for them. It isn't until you've moved far enough along the Experience Curve that your incremental costs become less than a sustainable selling price. Once you have reached this point of critical mass, all you need to do is listen to the needs of your customers and shape your products, and tangible or intangible services, to better meet those needs. Over time, you'll enhance existing offerings and develop new ones. Ideally, you develop products that appeal to both your current and your new markets.

Less is more

If you expect to successfully diversify, you must focus your exploration of new products and services. Consider the experience of a software company that was number one in its market niche, with the reputation and margins you would expect from exploiting their vast experience. Years earlier, the company's strategic planning team had identified the risk that their market niche could ultimately collapse as computer technology advanced. It was part of their strategy to develop additional markets to support the business when the core market started what was expected to be a gradual decline. Alas, they didn't recognize the importance of having on board an executive with the marketing acumen to lead the diversification effort. When the anticipated technology arrived, the market began to collapse, and the company started losing money. The board brought in a new president to turn the business around.

When Harper, the newly hired president chosen because of his marketing expertise, had his first meeting with the software company's executive team, he asked the obvious question. "Our core business is collapsing – which of our other businesses should we focus on to replace the revenue?" The marketing vice president, Jane, told Harper the company had plenty to choose from, since it was in sixteen other markets.

"That sounds promising," said Harper. "Tell me more about our financial market." Jane explained how the company had developed a financial product, taken out a full-page ad in the *Harvard Business Review*, and had a satisfied customer utilizing the product.

Upon hearing this, Harper delivered a jolt of reality: "Sounds like you have a financial customer, not a market. You don't have a market until you have multiple customers. From what I see, we don't really have a real product – just a custom application." In fact, after further review, it turned out that the company wasn't in sixteen other markets; it had sixteen customers utilizing sixteen custom applications. This shouldn't have been much of a surprise, since the company's focus had been custom development. The strategic failure was not recognizing the distinction between a custom application and a product, and between a customer and a market. To paraphrase Aristotle, "one customer does not a market make." The one market the company *was* in (the collapsing legacy market of custom development) didn't even have a product manager, a condition Harper quickly corrected. Proactively managing a legacy market can be the cash cow that funds development of successor markets. Running without a strategy or a leader, the company's collapsing legacy market was in fact burning cash.

Inspired by Harper's marketing insights, the executive team moved quickly. They decided on a strategy to "milk" the core business, generating sufficient cash to keep the company afloat. They put the executive most knowledgeable about the legacy business in charge and he quickly implemented the strategy. He shut down eighteen branch offices and sold off the European distributors. He ended the pointless new business sales activities as well as investments in product development geared to attract new customers to a technology the market had moved away from. He shifted the focus to retention of existing legacy clients by beefing up a small, centralized 24/7 support department and developing incremental product enhancements that extended customer retention and had a payback of one year or less.

With the core business product/market strategy in place, the executive team shifted to identifying the market(s) to bet on in the future. They selected the most promising eight markets and sold off, gave away, or shut down the other eight. Then they researched each of the remaining eight to identify the most promising ones. For each potential market they answered the four questions: *Is it real? Can we do it? Can we win? Is it worth it?*

After three months the team had whittled the list down to four. By the end of the year, there were two horses left in the race. Both were markets in which the company would be able to attract new customers. Both had high-value problems the company could develop products to solve. Both had sufficient growth potential to meet the company's five-year revenue and profit goals. Within five years, the company had successfully established itself as a leader in each of the two markets, having sold off the remaining legacy business to a dedicated group of old-timers who nurtured the remaining customers.

It became clear in the initial executive team discussions that there wasn't clarity about what constituted a market and what constituted a product. Harper made sure each executive was using the same definitions.

Market: any focus that defines a group of prospective customers with common, high-value problems that the company has the competency to solve, is a group large enough to support the company's growth needs, and is a group that can be reached with cost-effective communications.

Product: any solution that solves a customer's problem and can ultimately be provided at a cost less than the value the customer attaches to the solution. Products are the "excuse" the customer has for paying us. They can be packaged like a box of screws or delivered as a service like consulting.

Ten key elements of a product/market strategy

Your team should reach strategic agreement regarding each of the 10 major elements of a product/market strategy:

- Markets
- Products
- Geographic coverage
- Profit
- Pricing
- Market and product diversity
- Customer base size
- Partnerships

- Branding
- Exploration and exploitation

Markets

How many markets will you be in and what share of the five-year revenue are you targeting for each? For example, your company might say, "Within five years we will be 60 percent in consumer packaged goods, 30 percent in industrial, and 10 percent in a new market, likely specialty automotive or consumer medical."

Products

How many products will you provide and what is their share of your total revenue? For example, "We anticipate that 80 percent of our products will be closures with over half utilizing proprietary designs. The remaining 20 percent will be other custom products that fit our manufacturing capabilities."

Geographic coverage

What is your geographic focus for sales? Are you regional, focusing on customers in the Chicago or mid-Atlantic regions? Are you national, selling to companies based in all 50 U.S. states? Are you North American, covering the U.S., Canada, and Mexico? Are you international, selling to companies based around the world? Or, are you global, not only selling to companies worldwide but manufacturing and supporting them with local facilities? For example, shipping product to Germany for a U.S. company does not make you international. Selling to a German company and shipping to their customers' locations does.

Having a customer in Brazil that called you unsolicited for a sale in Brazil also doesn't fit the definition of international. (However, when several Brazilian companies start calling you to buy your products, it's a signal that it may be time to change your geographic strategy to proactively sell in Brazil.)

THE CHEMISTRY OF PRODUCT/MARKET STRATEGIES

> **Profit is a measure of the value we create from our stewardship of the resources under our management. Profit should never be seen as "what's left over." Profit should be engineered into the strategy.**

Profit

I have a philosophical view of profit. To me, profit is a measure of the value we create from our stewardship of the resources under our management. Profit should never be seen as "what's left over." Profit should be engineered into the strategy. Operationally, your budget should start with defining the yearly revenue and profit. Then allocate investments and expenses consistent with delivering those two numbers.

How much value-added do you require in your products? If your competitors average a 10 percent profit and your strategy is to create a 15 percent profit, where will that 5 percent come from? Products that address a customer's mission-critical problem are more valuable to the customer and can support a higher profit margin. (A $100,000 product that saves the customer $10,000 per month is easy for a customer to justify. It is irrelevant to them that it may only cost you $50,000 to deliver it.) Economies of scale – another aspect of the Experience Curve – can drive your costs down. If you purchase ten times as much raw material than your nearest competitor, you are likely to get substantially better terms from your vendor. Pump out ten times the volume from your plant and the overhead per product plummets. Location can be conducive to your business. Favorable local regulations, taxes, and a low cost of living can reduce your overhead. Being co-located with your largest customer can minimize coordination and shipping costs. (Microsoft's initial location was in Albuquerque, New Mexico, right across the street from Altair, the first personal computer manufacturer in the U.S.)

Pricing

Are you value-pricing your product based on the value received? It's natural to think of pricing a product as cost plus a reasonable profit. This concept has two flaws. One is that you can end up pricing your product out of the market. This is a point in favor of having a strategic loss leader. Brad, a new manager at a fine linens company, suggested that the company eliminate sheets from its product line. "At best, we break even on every sheet we sell. We make our money on pillow cases, shams, and matelassé bedspreads." "Are you crazy!" exclaimed the owner. "People buy bedding sets, and if we didn't sell sheets at cost, no one would buy our bedspreads."

The second flaw is leaving too much money on the table and losing the resources you could use to consolidate your market position. Take the 50 percent profit margin and reinvest it preparing for the inevitable onslaught of competitive products. Make sure that when a competitor tries to copy your product you have already created an enhanced one. If you are the lowest-cost provider, you can always reduce the price of a product and block your competitor from undercutting you by price. In practice, you seldom can increase your price so it's a better strategy to start high and bring the price down.

Another factor to keep in mind regarding pricing is what you tie your price to. Back in the 1970s, mainframe-based computer time-sharing services billed their customers based on their access to their centralized computer. They billed monthly for the number of minutes each customer's users were dialed into the computer, the mainframe CPU seconds those users consumed, and the bytes of data they stored. The educational and support services that actually created the customer value were provided free. When technology advanced to a point where customers could afford to purchase hardware themselves, they leaped to an obvious, albeit incorrect, conclusion that they were being ripped off because they could purchase an entire disk drive for one month's typical billing. Your pricing strategy should align *how* you charge with *where* the customer is actually receiving value. It is impossible to change a customer's perception of value after the fact. Your pricing strategy should create that perception from the start.

Market and product diversity

In Chapter 5 we discuss the danger of too much concentration (or putting all your eggs in one basket). In the words of Albert Einstein, you want to "make your focus as simple as possible but no simpler."

Customer base size

You should specify the number and target revenue you expect from each of your targeted customers. For example, a company might say: "We will support the business with five major customers, each generating at least $2.5 million in annual revenues, and fifty smaller customers, each with the potential to reach $2.5 million in annual sales." The design of your sales and support should be tailored to your customer base strategy.

Partnerships

What role do partnerships play in implementing your five-year strategy? What is your acquisition strategy? It could be as simple as "Hell no, we will never waste resources try to merge with another company's culture." It could be as opportunistic as "We'll consider acquisition opportunities brought to us that augment our strategy." Or, it could be an integral part of the strategy as in, "We will proactively seek one or two $5 million-dollar acquisitions of companies with a compatible culture that fit our strategy."

There is a full range of partnership relationships beyond the total consummation of an acquisition. You may choose to work with competitors to establish standards, use joint ventures to develop new technology, or do joint marketing in a new area. Just as in personal relationships, working with a company for several years can validate the value of a future merger.

Branding

Do you want to be invisible and fly under the radar? Companies that don't want to signal potential competitors often follow this branding strategy. Most small companies, and that means any company smaller than Amazon, Apple, or GM, need to project a "larger than life" market presence. That means aligning product names and brands with a common look and feel. Having a myriad of product names and brands diffuses that market presence. One of the smartest things Oracle Corporation did when they were a small company was to rename their company after their product and then incorporate that name in every one of their subsequent products. That way, any media articles written about the Oracle product also promoted the company.

Exploration and exploitation

Every strategy has a balance of exploitation and exploration. Once you have found the magic formula for success, the company's major focus should be exploitation of that formula.

Isaac shared war stories from the founding of his printing company. "During the first few years, we explored a half-dozen areas of specialty printing until we found our niche in the financial industry. Since then, we have focused on exploiting our growing dominance by sustaining business from eight to nine of the top ten financial institutions. That has been the secret of our success." Isaac's company explores a few non-financial opportunities every year just in case, but their strategy is dominated by exploitation of their current market niche.

Contrast that with the company described earlier in this chapter that found itself in a collapsing market and switched its focus so all hands, except for a rear-guard contingent, were intent on exploring new markets. Even when you have a solid core market with huge potential, devote some resources to exploration. It's a relatively cheap way to perform market research and can provide a head start if your core market stumbles.

In the next chapter, we'll discuss the chemistry of a healthy organization. How can you surround yourself with passionate, competent people who delight and amaze you daily? How can you build an organization where all you need to do is clearly state the results you need and they get implemented as if by magic? Implementing strategy, no matter how brilliant, requires an organization that is structured for success.

CHAPTER SUMMARY

The Chemistry of Product / Market Strategies

What are the major concepts in this chapter?

- You need a balance between exploitation and exploration. (That is, how much emphasis you place on consolidating your current position and how much on developing potential future sources of revenue.)
- You need a diversity of customers and products. (This helps you reduce the risk from losing a single customer or product, and balance it with the need to maximize the Experience Curve.)
- You need a focus that is sufficient to generate enough transactions so that you become the best at what you do. (Maximize the value of the Experience Curve.)
- You need an agreement on the role of partnerships. (Will you seek casual dating, platonic relationships, or corporate marriage?)
- You need to identify a targeted profitability. (Profit isn't what's left over, it's what you engineer it to be.)

Why are these major concepts important?

- Being the leader can be a license to print money.
- Handling today's success blinds us to product life cycles.

How can you apply these major concepts?

- Specify how you will achieve the targeted profit margin. For example, "We will increase margins by charging for added value, achieving economies of scale, utilizing lower cost raw materials, and outsourcing non-critical functions."
- Specify the future markets and their targeted revenue. For example, "We will focus on three markets: automotive at 60

percent of revenue, industrial at 30 percent, and a third, likely medical, at 8 percent. The remaining 2 percent will be from markets we test from time to time."

- Specify the future products and their share of total revenue and profit. For example, "We will focus on latches and fittings for 80 percent of our business, with 20 percent coming from a new line of carburetors."
- Specify the number of and expected revenues from your targeted customers. For example, "We will support the business with five major customers, each generating at least $2.5 million in annual business, and fifty smaller customers, each with the potential to reach another $2.5 million in annual sales."
- Specify the role of mergers and acquisitions and other partnerships. For example, "We will look to acquire one or two companies that fit our culture and strategy and add at least $5 million to our revenue."

Want more? Download a FREE workbook at myrna.com/books

Chapter 7
Organizing to Win

"Ability is what you're capable of doing. Motivation determines what you do. Attitude determines how well you do it."

Lou Holtz

"Concentrate all your thoughts upon the work at hand. The sun's rays do not burn until brought to a focus."

Alexander Graham Bell

I was sitting next to an airline pilot who was a passenger on a flight heading back to Providence, and we got to chatting about careers. Tom had been flying with the airline for 13 years and had flown 15 years for the Marines before that. I was surprised he had left the Marines so early, since five more years would have earned him a pension.

"I had joined as a calling but found myself thinking of it as just a job," Tom explained. "Further, I missed my son's third birthday and I didn't want to be an absentee father. I love flying but it was time for a change." Tom had recognized that he had lost his passion, and that the requirements of a Marine pilot deployed in Afghanistan did not align with his life needs. There wasn't anything wrong with Tom; he was simply in the wrong job at the wrong time.

Tom had zeroed in on two of the three factors that make the difference between top-performing employees and underperforming players who drag the whole organization down with them. The three factors are passion, alignment, and competence. Based on how well an employee and job fit together, they can be a catalyst for progress or a dead weight, not because they are "good" or "bad," but because they are in the right job or the wrong one.

> ## Chapter focus
>
> This chapter discusses hiring based on aptitude, attitude, and chemistry. Once hired, an individual's performance is driven by how closely their job ignites their passion, benefits from their competence, and aligns with their personal situation. The chapter offers models and simple tools to help you match a position's desired results and required authority levels with the proper candidates.

Bond the person and the job

In the chemistry of growth, the results are only as good as the people implementing the strategy. The ideal person in the right job at the critical time will produce superior results. Task the wrong person with the job and you can expect failure.

Employees in the right job act with *passion*. The requirements of the job are in *alignment* with their personal life, and they are exceptionally *competent*. (Competency is a natural outgrowth of pairing an individual's attitude and aptitude with a job that inspires passion and alignment.) The more instances of specific passion, alignment, and competence behaviors, the closer an employee is to being a star employee. The fewer examples of those behaviors, the closer an employee is to being a chronic headache.

Ideally, an employee would have the insight that Tom the pilot had shown, and initiate a move to a new job on their own. More often than not, the responsibility of making sure the right people are in the right jobs falls on management. Employee performance directly relates to their job fit.

Understanding your "Platinum" and "Lead"

We can apply the Pareto Principle (also known as the 80-20 Rule) to employee performance. Twenty percent of your employees typically create 80 percent of the value for your company, and a different 20 percent of your employees create 80 percent of your headaches. Taking this one step further, 20 percent of the 20 percent will deliver 80 percent of the 80 percent, i.e., 4 percent of the workforce produces 64 percent of the positive outcome in your company, and another 4 percent produces 64 percent of the negative impact. With these figures in mind, we created the Platinum Paradigm™ model to characterize the star performers (platinum) and nonperformers (lead) in an organization – but with an added twist

The Platinum Paradigm™

Employee performance will be platinum, gold, silver, bronze, tin, or lead based on how well the individual's **passion**, **competence**, and personal **alignment** matches their current job

4%	your super performers, self-actualized (the 20% of the 20%)	*platinum*
16%	your great performers – lavish rewards and attention on these folks	*gold*
30%	the core of steady performing folks	*silver*
30%	folks not quite with it - striving to improve or drifting lower	*bronze*
16%	folks just getting by - drifting lower or struggling to improve	*tin*
4%	folks trapped in a negative spiral, frustrating everyone	*lead*

Transition folks who are trapped in the wrong job for them - the organization's lead weights. Eliminating lead's negative energy motivates the tin and bronze to enhance their fit.
Alchemists wasted lives trying to transmute lead into gold – be a manager not an alchemist.

Platinum performers have *passion* for the job, are exceptionally *competent*, and their personal needs are perfectly *aligned* with the requirements of the job. Platinum players are so passionate about what they do that their work becomes a source of personal fulfillment and satisfaction. (As Confucius said: "Choose a job you love, and you will never have to work a day in your life.") The knowledge and skills they bring to their work can make them as much as a hundred times more productive than other workers. The requirements of their jobs match their personal needs for a work environment. Their jobs suit them perfectly. The metal platinum is a precious, powerful catalyst. Platinum performers can be powerful assets in an organization when used as a catalyst to accelerate implementation of your strategy.

> **There is an ebullience that follows getting the lead out of an organization.**

In direct contrast with your platinum-level performers, the lead-level workers lack the passion, personal alignment, and competence required to execute their current jobs. The lead-level employees may totally lack passion for their jobs for any number of reasons, including burnout, boredom, or a perceived lack of choice. The lead workers are incompetent in their jobs, sometimes because the jobs outgrew them. And, the personal needs of lead workers are out of alignment with the needs of the job. Employees who are lead performers aren't evil or bad; they are just trapped in the wrong jobs. (Lead is heavy and toxic. Lead-level performers drag others down and there is an ebullience that follows getting the lead out of an organization.)

The 92 percent of your workforce that lies between the two extremes of platinum and lead has some imperfect mix of passion, alignment, and competence. It is management's ongoing role to develop people and positions to optimize all three. Individual training and development programs only improve competence. Redefining positions and carefully selecting which people you put in those positions optimizes your use of individual passions and alignments.

A major word of caution here. There is a human resources management system called "forced rankings" that on its face appears similar to the Platinum Paradigm™. Execution of forced rankings, popularized by General Electric in the 1980s, could be as crude as firing 10 percent of the workforce every year. Whether by intent or not, pitting employees against each other can and has damaged teamwork and redirected individual employees to focus on promoting themselves rather than advancing the business. Remember your pledge never to do something stupid because of something written on a piece of paper. The percentages in the Platinum Paradigm™ model, while typical, will vary from company to company and from year to year. Focus on achieving the best bonding chemistry between employee and job position rather than filling an arbitrary annual quota for Lead or Tin performers.

Attitude and aptitude

When I was earning my electrical engineering degree, I was a member of an elite group of top students. We all had high grade point averages, but we all didn't have the same aptitude. Ray and James were brilliant — they only had to attend classes, skim the textbooks, and quickly finish their homework before driving home for the evening.

I paid my expenses by teaching the accordion, a business I purchased from my retiring instructor when I was a sophomore in high school. I also put in at least thirty hours a week studying. I wasn't as brilliant as Ray and James, but by putting in the hours I was able to compete with them. Jerry didn't have to work at a job, but he averaged the same thirty hours of studying to keep up with the rest of us.

Harry wasn't as smart as any of us, but still kept up by studying fifty hours a week. He was an excellent student and went on to have an exemplary electrical engineering career, largely because he was willing to put in whatever number of hours it took to match the performance of others who were more brilliant.

Ray went on to the Massachusetts Institute of Technology (MIT) for an advanced degree, but dropped out short of getting his PhD there because keeping up with the other brilliant students required too many study hours. He had superior aptitude but had not yet developed the attitude required to succeed at that level. There was a lack of "chemistry" between Ray and the MIT culture.

Over the years, I've learned from that example and countless others to put less emphasis on a potential employee's résumé and current skills. Instead, I've found success when I hired someone with a reasonable aptitude and the right attitude. With the right attitude, such a new hire might have to initially work over 60 hours a week to deliver the same results as a more seasoned employee. But such a person would be more than willing to invest the extra 20 hours to come up to speed. (Once up to speed, the new hire could deliver the same results in the same nominal 40-hour work week.)

Employees with the right attitude view the extra hours as their personal investment in achieving the goals they set for themselves. While you may think that the superior employee is one who on day one can achieve the desired results in the "normal" work week, they aren't, necessarily. When there is a new challenge in your business or a new skill set is required for a job, which employee is most likely to rise to the occasion because he or she already has the established habit of investing extra time to come up to speed?

"People chemistry" matters

Have you ever found yourself in a situation where you wondered what you did wrong in hiring someone? At one of my companies, we prescreened all candidates carefully and did multiple interviews. We had everyone who would be working with the top candidate, Dale, talk with him and make sure the fit was right. We double-checked all of Dale's references. I even made sure that I understood his personal goals for the next five years and was confident he could reach them in our company. After two years of trying, I finally threw in the towel and fired him – to the relief of both of us. What did we miss? In a word, chemistry.

HR professionals have told me that as a rule of thumb, you need to hire three people for every two that you end up keeping. This ratio assumes that you have an excellent hiring process. Why can't we "get it right" 100 percent of the time? The answer is chemistry. Until an employee is functioning in the actual job, neither they nor you can be sure of the fit.

For hiring, I recommend a 90-day "warranty" period. If the job fit doesn't feel right within that period for you or the employee, chances are it won't ever be right. It isn't fair to the misfit employee or his teammates to keep trying to make it work out. "Hire slowly, fire quickly" is the motto of successful managers.

The chemistry, or lack thereof, between the individuals implementing your company's strategy can produce grand success or blow the organization up. When there is chemistry in a relationship, people can talk about anything and everything. They have the same values and purpose, and share the same long-term goals. Your people are ultimately the ones who will implement your strategy. Without organizational chemistry, they can't or won't hear, understand, and embrace the strategy. Without supportive interpersonal chemistry, they won't be able to develop the "*how*" of the strategy and be empowered to execute it.

Hire based on aptitude (having enough grey matter to master the skills), and attitude (the passion and commitment to put in the time to master the required skills). Once you've done that, assess the third key factor, chemistry, the critical secret ingredient in the hiring process.

The right chemistry

It isn't enough to hire the right people, you need to form a strong bond between the right people and the right positions. The right jobs for *them*. The better the match, the stronger the bonding chemistry. This starts with defining the requirements of the job. It's common to approach the process of creating a job description in terms of the tasks the employee is expected to perform and then create a recruiting description based on years of education and experience. Instead, ask yourself what are the required and ideal levels of authority required by the job. What are the five or so most important results the employee is responsible for creating? For each of the major responsibilities, what is the level of authority they will have to be trusted with in order to smoothly fulfill their role in the company? (Take a look at the Authority Table™ below to see how this works.) Then make sure that the candidate for the position has sufficient competence to warrant the required authority and sufficient aptitude and attitude to progress to the ideal level.

Authority Table™

Levels of authority for each responsibility each level of **authority** derives from demonstrated, or assumed, **competence**	1 *Wait* until told what to do	2 **Ask** for direction	3 **Suggest** action	4 **Tell** after acting	5 **Empowered** to act independently
Responsibility 1				√	
Responsibility 2				√	
Responsibility 3			√		
Responsibility 4			√		
Responsibility 5		√			

√ Identifies minimum authority/competence required to fulfill each responsibility

Tracking authority and responsibility

Level 1. Wait until told what to do is the lowest level of authority. The employee is not expected to even recognize when action is required. During one of the joint American-Russian missions on the Russian space station Mir, the two Russian cosmonauts had to go on a space walk, leaving the American astronaut on board. His instructions were simple: "Sit on your hands and don't touch anything until or unless we tell you exactly what to do." The risk of his acting independently, even with his training, was too high.

Level 2. Ask for direction is the second-lowest level of authority. An employee is expected to recognize that action is required and seek direction from their manager. Locating the manager, asking for direction, and understanding the manager's decision all take time. The requirement for a manager's participation creates a bottleneck, suggesting that time-critical responsibilities require an employee in this position with the competence to warrant a higher level of authority than this.

Level 3. Suggest action is the middle level of authority. At this level the employee is expected to not only recognize that action is required but be able to suggest what actions could be taken. While a step up from asking for direction, the requirement for a manager's decision still leaves the bottleneck in place.

Level 4. Tell after acting is the second-highest level of authority. The employee is expected to recognize that action is required and has the competence and judgment to take satisfactory action. Not requiring permission to act eliminates his manager as a bottleneck. Requiring him to inform his manager about his action provides an opportunity for his manager to review the action and suggest what might be an even better approach the next time a similar issue comes up. The manager is no longer a potential bottleneck.

Level 5. Empowered to act independently is the highest level of authority. The employee is trusted to make quality decisions, knowing when he should check with management. The manager is freed to focus on other aspects of the business.

For the most important responsibilities of a position, the candidate has to be trusted to execute their job at Level 4 or 5 in order for the organization to function smoothly. A salesman must be able to interact with a prospect without making unachievable commitments. An operator must be able to run his press without damaging the tool. For other responsibilities it may be acceptable to operate at a lower authority level. A new manager, for example, might have to run prospective personnel changes by her manager first (Level 3 or 2). For annual budgeting, it might even be acceptable to have someone wait until told what action was required. The key concept is that different responsibilities within a job can and should have different levels of authority. The levels of authority should be communicated clearly. When an employee asks why they have to check with you for some decisions when they don't for others, explain what competence they have yet to prove to warrant that level of authority, and how they can earn it.

Authority is earned by the employee's demonstrated competence. To be worthy of being hired for new positions, having more meaningful work delegated to them, or being promoted, employees must have the competence to exercise a high level of authority for their major responsibilities, which comprise, usually, a minimum number of "***tell after acting***" and "***empowered***" responsibilities. Other activities can function at a lower authority level, i.e., at the "***ask***," and, ideally, "***suggest***" levels. An organization can't function if too many individuals are in positions where they need to **wait until told** what to do. (One of the two reasons I'd fire a manager on the spot was when they consistently hired people dumber than they were. If those hires in time hired even dumber people, eventually I'd have an organization of idiots waiting to be told what to do next.) Remember the pledge to not do something stupid because of a piece of paper – emphasize sensibleness over procedures.

If you have someone you can't trust with the minimum level of authority the job requires, you must act. Resize the job or replace the employee with someone who can operate at that level.

Create a bond between the right people and the right position

"It's my fault. If I had spent more time with him or if we had a better training program I'm sure he wouldn't need the supervision I have to give him." Ashley was talking about Jay, who just couldn't be trusted to act on his own. "He is taking up hours of my time. We've missed a couple of customer deadlines already because I was tied up and he couldn't move ahead until I told him what to do." Ashley had a problem but it wasn't the one she thought she had. The problem wasn't that her company didn't have a training program like Intel or General Electric. No company the size of hers could support such a training program. The problem wasn't that she didn't spend more time with the new hire. She invested even more time than the average manager at her company. The problem was that she had hired the wrong person.

Her company wasn't a corporate giant, it was a $10 million dollar firm with under seventy-five employees. By necessity, all its employees were required to have the competence to fulfill their primary responsibilities by acting independently or with regular, after-the-fact, reviews. They didn't need a better training program; they weren't large enough to sustain the quality of such a program. They needed a better recruitment and on-boarding program. They implemented such a strategy with elements to:

- Clarify the minimum level of authority required by the major responsibilities of each position.
- Identify the verifiable competence required to warrant that level of authority.
- Sustain a pre-employment screening process that verifies a candidate's experience and competence to operate at that level.
- Sustain a pre-employment screening process that validates the candidate's alignment with the job requirements.
- Have an on-boarding process that quickly gets the new employee productive.
- Have a clear 90-day warranty period to validate chemistry. They became ruthless about cutting their losses and letting go the one out of three hires that wouldn't work out. They count the 90-day cuts as part of the cost of recruitment rather than letting it affect their retention metrics.

Sustain a diverse workforce

"We have virtually zero turnover. Most of our managers have been with us over thirty years." Carlos, the HR director, was bragging. "We do have a problem, however. Most of them will be retiring within five to ten years and we don't have many strong middle managers." Milt, the sales manager, added an insight on the impact of all the managers being from the same generation. "The salespeople I hire don't seem to return my telephone calls. I had to get a smart phone and learn how to text. Otherwise I'd never be able to communicate with them when they're out of the office. I'm concerned that we don't understand what this new generation is all about. Plus, more of our prospective customers and employees are from different ethnic backgrounds we don't seem to be able to connect to."

Healthy organizations have a steady influx of new employees who inject new experiences, concepts, and technology and a culture that develops people through strategic delegation. You can enhance short-term results by always leaning on the old reliable employees and never recruiting, developing, and promoting younger ones. However, at some point your old employees will burn out, retire, or die.

The next chapter covers the strategic need for continuous improvement of quality, process, and people. Companies don't exist in a vacuum. Every year competitors, vendors, and customers get smarter, new technologies get introduced, and everyone seems to want everything cheaper, better, faster. If you don't have a proactive strategy for continuous improvement, then by default you're not standing still, you're falling behind.

CHAPTER SUMMARY
Organizing to Win

What are the major concepts in this chapter?
- A healthy workforce needs to be diverse in ages, backgrounds, and experience.
- Employees will be bronze, tin, or lead performers based on their negative passion, competence, and personal alignment with their job.
- Employees will be platinum, gold, or silver performers based on their positive passion, competence, and personal alignment with their job.
- Positions can be defined by the levels of authority each of the job's responsibilities require to function smoothly.
- The right people have the right mix of aptitude, attitude, and chemistry.

Why are these major concepts important?
- The key to becoming a great company is not only to hire and retain the right people but to form a strong bond between the right people and the right positions.

How can you apply these major concepts?
- Develop and deploy an effective strategy for recruiting and retaining people with the right aptitude, attitude, and chemistry.
- Structure job descriptions based on the most important results the job holder is expected to deliver and the level of authority required to smoothly execute each responsibility.

Want more? Download a FREE workbook at myrna.com/books

Like this book? Please leave a review at Amazon.com!

Chapter 8
Productivity and Continuous Improvement

"If you don't have time to do it right, when will you have time to do it over?"

John Wooden

"Experience is not what happens to a man; it is what a man does with what happens to him."

Aldous Huxley

The strategic planning meeting started on a downbeat note. "We may have to dissolve the partnership." Arturo, the president of the AMG Medical Group, was reviewing the potential impact of next year's huge jump in their malpractice insurance premium. Their insurance agent had put it simply: With the number of lawsuits the firm faced last year, what did they expect? "But the lawsuits have been without merit, including the one we lost," protested Julia, their practice manager. "It doesn't matter," Arturo said. "We can expect our premiums to continue to increase and put us out of business unless something changes." "What can we do?" Julia asked. The answer was to set a strategic goal to change the status quo by dramatically increasing the quality of their patient management. AMG's quality issues were threatening their very existence.

I asked the group, "What are the root causes that ultimately led to the big lawsuit you lost?" It boiled down to three reasons:

Clocks: The clocks in the medical facility were not synchronized with each other, which created the illusion that procedures were not being followed. The jury decided that AMG's physician was lying when the times recorded on the patient's chart didn't match the testimony.

Lack of follow-up: They hadn't followed up the next day once the patient had been discharged. The overworked physician's assistant didn't have a reliable system for verifying that anyone had actually spoken with the patient. A patient who should have been told to return right away for additional treatment showed up days later with serious complications.

Wrong physician: The physician who handled the patient was always "too busy" to document procedures, making it impossible to effectively defend the practice in court. She also was too busy to establish a trusting relationship with her patients. While she was a passionate, competent physician, she was not aligned with the non-medical demands of the job.

AMG set and implemented strategic goals to methodically identify every root cause, develop a solution, and implement it. The physician who was too busy didn't have her contract renewed. The clocks were upgraded to maintain synchronization. The patient follow-up system was enhanced with additional staffing to guarantee 100 percent compliance.

AMG also set and implemented a system to continuously identify where else similar quality issues might exist and apply their solutions to those areas. They chose to not renew the contract of two other physicians whose patient feedback identified them as "untrustworthy." They upgraded their physician recruitment process to add "warm and friendly" to their hiring criteria. They also enhanced other feedback systems to guarantee 100 percent compliance.

Once their insurance carrier was satisfied that AMG had indeed changed the status quo, AMG experienced annual reductions in their premiums. Further, the changes led to greater patient retention and referrals.

Just as important as fixing the specific issues that led to their losing the lawsuit, AMG instituted a cultural change that emphasized continuous improvement across the entire practice. Physicians had always practiced continuous improvement within the narrow scope of their specialty. The change in status quo was to spread that culture across all aspects of the business. AMG identified opportunities to increase productivity, formed small teams to focus on an opportunity, and over time were able to double their profitability. As importantly, they made themselves more valuable to the hospitals who utilized their services, negotiating long-term contracts that provided greater stability for the practice.

> **Chapter focus**
>
> This chapter discusses why continuous improvement and reducing the cost of poor quality is an essential element of strategy. It has been estimated that as much as 40 percent of annual revenue gets lost fixing faulty products, hiring the wrong people, pursuing the wrong customers, delaying receiving payment because of incomplete information, etc. Continuous improvement concepts can be applied across all industries and across all elements of your business.

The cost of poor quality

The commonly used term "cost of quality" is a measure of the total cost of *not* creating a quality product. Every time work is redone, the cost of quality increases. Not only does the cost of quality reduce profitability, it creates frustration. Nothing negatively impacts motivation more than seeing your hard work tossed into the garbage.

There is a well-developed process for reducing the cost of quality – it's called root cause analysis. While there are many detailed steps in a formal implementation of the process, the key is to establish a culture that continuously drives down to the root cause of every quality issue, and then ruthlessly neutralizes it. Simply stated, root cause analysis has three steps:

1. *What* is the problem, including the qualitative and quantitative properties of the harm it does?
2. *Why* did it happen, and can you identify the causal factors that directly resulted in the effect?
3. *How* can you prevent this from happening again, applying the solutions not only to the specific issue that triggered the analysis but to all other similar potential problems?

> **Continuous improvement is a state of mind and an attitude.**

The culture of continuous improvement

Continuous improvement is more than a buzzword, although it's often used that way. It doesn't require formal training and systems, although these can be of value when you can afford them. Continuous improvement is a state of mind and an attitude. Closely coupled with the Experience Curve, it is the cultural norm that demands and expects everyone to seek a better way to do everything.

Manufacturers routinely invest in lean manufacturing systems such as Six Sigma and Kaizen in support of continuous improvement of production. Continuous improvement systems inspired by lean manufacturing can be applied to all aspects of a business. Each of the lean manufacturing implementation processes isn't all that hard to visualize. You identify an opportunity for improvement and form a team to work on the strategic quality objective. Then each team "swarms" – has quick, focused meetings – periodically to sustain momentum until an objective is achieved. Like chemists, they return from the field to their laboratory to examine the field data, test their theories, and plan the next experiment.

The laboratory sessions accelerate progress by having the team complete four steps.

Assessment: A disciplined assessment by the team on a regular basis informs an agreement on adjustments to the tactical action plans. What did we learn from the last set of action steps? Did anyone recognize an opportunity for a better way to move ahead? On completion of the project, the team and stakeholders determine and document what actual impact the project had compared to the objectives set at the project's start.

Agreement: Reach agreement with all the stakeholders on what success will look like when the team finishes the project. This includes measures of quality, quantity, timeliness, and cost. Reach agreement on why those outcomes are valuable enough to invest the team's resources, and on how the team intends to achieve those outcomes. Make sure everyone understands what the next steps are.

Accountability: Establish accountability with clear roles, responsibilities, and authorities for every team member. Also establish accountability for completing specific tactical action steps within the agreed-upon timeframe. What is each team member's role in the next step – what are they accountable for?

Action: Focus on actions defined and completed within one to ninety days that are sufficient to achieve the agreed-upon outcomes. The meeting ends, and the team executes – with or without a tactical success. As Robert Kiyosaki says, "sometimes you succeed…. and other times you learn."

And then…they return to the lab and do it all over again.

I use a graphic, The Progress Accelerator™, to highlight the swarming process. The Progress Accelerator™ is a catalyst in the chemistry of growth.

The swarming team should change over time. The first swarm of a continuous improvement project should include all the stakeholders to make sure everyone agrees on the definition of a successful conclusion. Once there is clarity on what constitutes success, the core implementers swarm as frequently as necessary to sustain momentum, coordinate actions, and incorporate lessons learned.

Swarming was key to my success in completing a turnaround of a company losing $50,000 per month with less than $100,000 in the bank. For a month, every morning before work, the turnaround team swarmed for fifteen minutes to assess our current financial position, agree on what bills we would pay today, what receivables we would accelerate, and what sales we would push to close. As the cash flow crisis abated, we reduced the swarming frequency to a couple of times a week. After a quarter of positive cash flow, we had our final meeting to document lessons learned for the next time a crisis like this occurred.

External drivers

"You don't understand, John, in this market our customers are constantly raising expectations and expecting price givebacks. If we can't deliver the quality and cost improvement they demand, there are competitors who will." The CEO was giving me some background on his company before the strategic planning meeting. I smiled, since I've heard the same story from just about every company I've worked with.

Every year, his company, his competition, and his industry/market had the opportunity to get smarter from an additional twelve months of experience. Customers expect to see that experience reflected in reduced prices or more quality and features for the same price. (Sometimes, they expect both.) That means your company strategy must include a roadmap for how you will sustain annual improvements in competitiveness. In the case of this CEO's market, the productivity driver was external and explicit. His company's clients actually had annual givebacks in their contract. The contract specified specific annual improvements in quality and price. The company strategy was simple. Put continuous improvement programs in place that consistently delivered the contracted improvements in productivity.

Internal drivers

We have found that asking people to "improve things as much as you can" doesn't work as well as setting a specific, measurable goal and requiring the team to develop the tactical approach to hit it. You need to set those goals with care, considering what message you may be sending, as one of our clients found out to their dismay.

"It was hard, but we hit this month's target." Gene, the director of operations, was bragging. The directors of sales and finance were not impressed, and asked why customers didn't get their products on time, and why the company didn't make a profit. Why, indeed! Gene's response was classic.

"Those problems were because of the product mix. In order to make our target, we needed to prioritize the high-volume jobs which happened to have lower profit. In fact, some of them even lost money. This job mix was the only way to meet our monthly production quota."

To paraphrase Shakespeare, "the fault, dear Gene, is not in our stars, but in ourselves." The fault lies in the definition of the target rather than its execution. After the company changed targets to prioritize achieving profit while maintaining on-time delivery, it increased both profit and sales. Sales went up because on-time delivery led to higher sales, and meeting the profit target led to sales that improved the job mix so as to maximize profitability rather than volume.

You know the old management maxim, "what gets measured, gets done." Ask yourself what employees are being asked to do with these three common targets: revenue per full-time employee, minimum profit per product, and conventional sales commission plans.

- Setting a target to focus on **revenue per full-time employee** can lead to counterproductive hiring strategies. Managers will hire more expensive temps rather than full-time employees that would reduce their revenue/employee target. A better target is revenue per compensation dollar. Optimizing that metric leads managers to get the most productivity from their overall labor costs.

- Setting a target to maintain a **minimum profit per product** can lead to ignoring sales opportunities that would increase cash flow. As Eliyahu Goldratt discusses in his classic *The Goal: A Process of Ongoing Improvement*, accountants define profit as variable cost plus an allocation of your fixed costs charged to all your products. In fact, once you have enough revenue to cover your fixed costs, every dollar of incremental revenue, minus the cost to produce it, drops to the bottom line. If overhead accounts for 20 percent of a product's "cost," then selling excess capacity at a 15 percent discount can actually make a larger contribution to profit than your regular high-margin business.

- The **conventional sales commission plan** can lead to an unhealthy focus on selling exclusively to existing customers, to the detriment of acquiring new ones. It also tempts salespeople to maximize their compensation by offering discounts to pull in next year's sales. This often leads to a lower margin on year-end sales and a flat to negative next quarter.

People productivity

As we learned in Chapter 7, if you bond the right people to the right jobs, you will see platinum-level performance. However, over time, people's passion, competence, and alignment can change. An unmarried international VP may have loved traveling the world and being away from home three weeks a month. After finding and marrying the love of his life, he may find that job suddenly out of alignment with his new passion.

Continuous improvement of the bond between employees and their jobs can have the greatest impact on the success of a company. As part of the annual performance review, managers can perform a simple audit of each employee.

Passion for the job: positive, neutral, or negative.

Competence for the job: positive, neutral, or negative.

Alignment with the job: positive, neutral, or negative

Employee	Competence	Passion	Alignment	Next steps
Bob	Positive	Positive	Positive	Utilize on more taskforces
Carol	Neutral	Positive	**Negative**	Adjust hours of job
Migael	Positive	**Negative**	Positive	Put on new products team
Jack	**Negative**	Neutral	Positive	Send to school
Mildred	**Negative**	**Negative**	**Negative**	Transition out of company

The follow-up, based on the results of the audit, should be focused on moving the employee to the positive category for competence, passion, and alignment. Improvement usually involves both employee action and changes to his job.

For employees whose bonds with their jobs have been irreparably compromised, the compassionate and appropriate action is to quickly help them move to another position where they have the potential to be silver, gold, or platinum performers. At most small companies, that means a position at a new company. Managers often hesitate to move the "Mildreds" due to a false sense of compassion. Everyone knows Mildred is failing. Keeping her in a failing job is sucking out her soul. It is substantially better for both Mildred and the company to demonstrate compassion through a generous severance package and assistance in locating a new and better job. In the right job, everyone can excel. The cost of quality of retaining a lead-level employee cannot be overstated.

Bottom line

It's easy to be swayed by the romance of revenue. I explain the importance of continuous improvement and keeping unnecessary costs out of a business this way. Ask what your after-tax margin is and then explain how many dollars in new business you have to sell in order to generate an additional $10,000 in profit. If your margin is 10 percent, your company has to create, sell and deliver an additional $100,000 of product over and over again. The five-year net present value of the shop floor team reducing the cost of a process by $1,000 per month[6] is around $70,000. At a 10 percent profit margin, their accomplishment adds as much value to the company as a one-time $700,000 sale.

In the next chapter we discuss implementation. Vision without implementation is more than a waste of time. It breeds cynicism. Cynicism leads to the "everyone's in it for themselves" mindset. People ask how what they're doing today will benefit themselves, co-workers, and department independent of the impact on the company as a whole. Cynics don't waste their time asking how what they are doing today will help your company achieve its vision.

---

6   NPV calculated as $12,000/year for five years with a 1.5% discount rate.

CHAPTER SUMMARY
Productivity and Continuous Improvement

What are the major concepts in this chapter?

- Between 25 and 40 percent of annual revenue gets chewed up by the cost of poor quality. The cost of quality encompasses not only fixing faulty products, it also includes hiring the wrong people, pursuing the wrong customers, delaying receiving payment because of incomplete information, etc.
- Continuous improvement concepts can be applied across all industries and across all elements of your business.
- Continuous improvement is an essential element of the chemistry of growth.
- Continuous improvement of people is a key element of continuous improvement.

Why are these major concepts important?

- To remain competitive, a company has to improve at or faster than the industry average.
- With a year's experience, customers, competitors, and the industry/market get smarter, raising expectations for lower prices and/or greater value.

How can you apply these major concepts?

- Develop a culture of continuous improvement.
- Establish a productivity improvement goal in your strategy. For example, "We will reduce the average cost of production by 5 percent annually."
- Track a cost of quality metric that accurately portrays your progress.
- Keep developing employees and jobs and improving the match between the two.

Want more? Download a FREE workbook at myrna.com/books

Like this book? Please leave a review at Amazon.com!

Chapter 9
The Chemistry of Implementation

"Vision without execution is hallucination."
Thomas A. Edison

"Once you have established the goals you want and the price you're willing to pay, you can ignore the minor hurts, the opponent's pressure and the temporary failures."
Vince Lombardi

"How did you do it? What's your secret?" I had just finished facilitating the assessment segment of the client's strategic plan. They had been exceptionally successful in implementing their strategic goals. The CFO who was championing the strategic plan that year said, "Well, in reality, there were a few simple things we did that seemed to work:

"We shared with our middle managers *what* we were looking to accomplish this year and *why*. We then worked with them to determine *how* we would achieve those objectives.

"We made sure there was a single, named individual who was responsible to account for *where* we were, *why* we were there, and *what* future actions were planned to achieve the objective. (A named individual for each strategic goal, key result measure, and each action step.)

"We aggressively delegated sub-tasks to free up enough resources for people to prioritize the parts of the plan they were personally accountable for.

"Each responsible individual formed a working team that met on an ongoing basis. In each meeting they took stock of where they were, reached agreement on what the next actions were and who would be accountable for each.

"And then, we just did it."

Chapter focus

This chapter discusses straightforward approaches for successful, effective implementation. At the core is a need for personal accountability resting with individuals who understand what's strategically important to do and why it's valuable to the company and themselves to do it, who know how to actually do it, and who have a system to keep them on track. Implementation always impacts and involves multiple people who need to "swarm" periodically to coordinate through a cycle of assessment, agreement, accountability, and action. The ongoing challenge is to keep everyone focused on the right tasks while repeatedly communicating and connecting the dots between today's action steps and the company's visualized future. Strategic delegation can free up resources to use on implementing strategy.

Implementation definition

The dictionary definition of implementation is

> *"The process of putting a decision or plan into effect; execution.*
>
> *For example:*
>
> *"She was responsible for the implementation of the plan."*

The implementation process isn't all that hard to visualize. Form teams to work on the various strategic objectives. Then have each team "swarm" periodically to sustain momentum until an objective is achieved. Like chemists, implementers periodically return to their laboratory from the field to examine the field data, test their theories, and plan the next experiment. (See The Progress Accelerator™ in Chapter 8 for more discussion of the swarming cycle of assessment, agreement, accountability, and action.)

> **Executives don't get paid to plan, they get paid to implement. Planning and the plan are the means to an end, not the end in itself.**

The strategic plan is your company's road map of what the planning team decided to focus on accomplishing. The challenge is how to translate those decisions into doing. As I remind every executive team I've ever worked with, executives don't get paid to plan, they get paid to implement. Planning and the plan are the means to an end, not the end in itself.

There are four enablers of successful implementation. The people you are counting on to implement the plan must do the following:

Understand that this is what the leadership really wants. In a busy environment where people are constantly being asked to do things, your requests must stand out.

Believe that this is the right thing for them to prioritize and do. Dedicated employees prioritize the things they know are in the best interests of the company, not the things a sometimes clueless management asks them to.

Know how to do it. They must have sufficient competence, time, and resources.

Have a system that keeps them on track, captures and reflects lessons learned, and keeps them on the same page with every stakeholder.

Let's take a closer look at each of these four implementation "enablers."

Understand it's what leadership really wanted

The written strategic business plan is the primary vehicle for communicating what the leadership really wants. It needs to be understood and supported by the company's CEO and leadership team and communicate specific objectives in a crystal-clear manner. However, people pay more attention to what their leaders do than what they say. Setting deadlines, having regular follow-up, and establishing positive and negative consequences all speak louder than words. The old chestnut "what gets measured gets done" speaks to this adage. Senior managers can have a surprising impact by simply popping into someone's office and asking how things are going on their project.

Sharing war stories, a venture capitalist colleague told me about a company he invested in that wasn't achieving the objectives outlined in their strategic business plan. After observing the company's president for several days, he had his answer. The president was directing a steady stream of ideas, suggestions, and requests at his employees. Important and unimportant requests were all presented with identical passion and lack of follow-up. The constant flurry of hundreds of requests had became little more than noise to the staff. The company got back on track once the venture capitalist "encouraged" the president to focus on communicating the company's handful of strategic objectives instead of his every random thought.

Believe it's the right thing to do

People resist acting when they do not see the value of the action. Corporate culture determines what is truly important. When your objectives align with employees' beliefs about what is important, the employees have no problem giving these objectives priority and implementing them. When there is misalignment, you need to shift beliefs and force a new prioritization on their part.

Consider a printing company that for decades made its profits by running big jobs for large financial institutions. Every employee knew that the way to guarantee success for the company and earn their annual bonus was to optimize big jobs. The big jobs amortized the substantial set-up and teardown costs inherent with silk-screen printing. Then the market changed and the majority of available jobs were from smaller financial institutions with jobs only one-tenth the size of those from the big firms. The sales team worked to sell ten times as many jobs to keep volume up. The production people, however, were still prioritizing based on what they knew was the most profitable, i.e. big jobs. Every time the sales team brought in a new customer with a small job, the production people put it at the bottom of the queue – doing what they *knew* was in the best interests of the company.

Unfortunately there will not be a second job when the first job for a new customer is delivered late. In order for the printing company to implement their strategic business plan, they had to re-educate their production people so they understood that small jobs had to become as much of a priority as big jobs. They also had to support that change by investing in new equipment and processes that enabled them to run small jobs profitably.

Your measurement and compensation system must align with your strategic business plan. If your plan is to diversify the customer base, the sales commission plan needs to reward more than total revenue. Calling on new customers drops to the bottom of sales reps' to-do list when the sales team *knows* that the only thing that counts is meeting the monthly revenue target.

Know how to do it

Matching a task to the people with the best mix of passion and competence is a key management skill. The people tasked with the job need to **want** to do it, understand **why** it is strategic to do, and know **how** to do it. Competence can vary as much as a hundred-to-one based on aptitude and experience. An employee can gain the required competence if he has exceptional passion for a task and sufficient aptitude to learn. Such a person may have to work twice as hard to get the job done, but will do so willingly because it is an opportunity for growth.

No one is sitting around waiting for something to do. Internal candidates with the competence to implement may not be available to take on a new task. This is an opportunity to review where people are spending their time and take advantage of delegation to free up resources. (Tactical approaches for effective delegation are discussed later in this chapter.)

Have a system to follow

Implementation is a four-phase cycle of agreement, accountability, action, and assessment. Let's have another look at the Progress Accelerator™.

Creating a virtuous cycle accelerates implementation while reducing the waste and quality declines that come with poor communications.

(1.) Agreement is the first phase in the cycle. It is necessary to agree on the priority of issues, tactical approach, and expected outcomes among the appropriate stakeholders. At a strategic level, this agreement is best reached between the CEO and the executive leadership team. At a tactical level, reaching this agreement can be as simple as the huddle that American football players hold before every play.

To implement, you need consensus and commitment from the implementers. *Consensus* is reached when every member of the implementation team agrees that the implementation plan makes sense. It may not be exactly what they would do if it was up to them exclusively, but it makes sense for the company. If it does not make sense for the company, then they need to keep working on the plan until it does. *Commitment* comes from a belief that this task is worth doing.

Real consensus and commitment are achieved when the implementation team members have voiced and worked through their concerns and misgivings prior to a team decision that all will support in public. Commitment is achieved through stages:

- Trust within a team enables people to be open.
- When people are open, they express their doubts and misgivings.
- When they express and have worked through their doubts and misgivings, they feel they were party to the final decision.
- When they feel party to the decision, they can commit to it.
- When they commit to the decision, they can commit to the implementation plan.

(2) Accountability refers to personal accountability or responsibility for completing a task and producing the agreed-upon outcome. Whether for a tactical action step or a key result measure, one (and only one) person must be designated to be accountable. There will always be multiple people involved, but without a single point of accountability you get the situation that "A poem about responsibility" relates so effectively.

Everybody, Somebody, Anybody, and Nobody
There was a most important job that needed to be done,
And no reason not to do it, there was absolutely none.
But in vital matters such as this, the thing you have to ask
Is who exactly will it be who'll carry out the task?

Anybody could have told you that **Everybody** knew
That this was something **Somebody** would surely have to do.
Nobody was unwilling; **Anybody** had the ability.
But **Nobody** believed that it was their responsibility.

It seemed to be a job that **Anybody** could have done,
If **Anybody** thought he was supposed to be the one.
But since **Everybody** recognized that **Anybody** could,
Everybody took for granted that **Somebody** would.

But **Nobody** told **Anybody** that we are aware of,
That he would be in charge of seeing it was taken care of.
And **Nobody** took it on himself to follow through,
And do what **Everybody** thought that **Somebody** would do.

When what **Everybody** needed so did not get done at all,
Everybody was complaining that **Somebody** dropped the ball.
Anybody then could see it was an awful crying shame,
And **Everybody** looked around for **Somebody** to blame.

Somebody should have done the job
And **Everybody** should have,
But in the end **Nobody** did
What **Anybody** could have.

— Charles Osgood, Former host of CBS Sunday Morning

(3) Action is tactical. It is a burst of activity that moves us closer to the desired outcome. One person is personally accountable for making sure it happens within a specified time period. Texas Instruments called this the W3 model:

- *What* will get done – a burst of activity that moves us closer to the objective
- *Who* will be accountable to make it happen – the catalyst and record keeper
- *When* will it be completed – the drop-dead date for completion

As Alec Mackenzie said in *The Time Trap*, his classic book on time management, "A goal without a deadline is just a dream."

Ninety days is the window for tactical action. Focusing on the actions that will actually get done this week, this month, and this quarter keeps execution real.

> **People do not naturally connect the dots. As often as not, they attribute success to luck or some other random event.**

(4) Assessment is accomplished in a review meeting. Tactical actions can be assessed during a daily, weekly, or monthly meeting that starts with a question about what we may have learned from previous actions, discussions, reading, etc. Strategically, the senior leadership team needs to close out the year's strategic goals during an annual two-day meeting. Closing last year's goals requires that management identify where the status quo has actually changed, and evaluate the success at achieving goals. The close-out should be communicated with the rest of the organization. This "connects the dots" between this year's accomplishments and previous years' planning. People do not naturally connect the dots. As often as not, they attribute success to luck or some other random event. "We couldn't have planned for that big sale, we were just lucky to have been in front of the customer when they were making a decision with a new product that just happened to exactly meet their emerging need." As the very lucky Thomas Jefferson is quoted as saying,

"I'm a great believer in luck, and I find the harder I work the more I have of it."

A client company in the pharmaceutical market had a core business of performing one-time development work. The backlog of business was never more than 90 days. In their strategic business plan, they set a goal to obtain recurring business to mitigate year-to-year revenue volatility. In a quarterly review meeting, the sales manager announced that he was delaying his proposal to win a big recurring contract because manufacturing was very busy. There was much discussion about the many issues that would have to be dealt with to win and deliver on the contract. It was clear that the current approach would not succeed. The team shifted into crisis mode and identified the company's biggest challenges. Each challenge had a single accountable owner and drop-dead date for completion. The president established a short meeting to be held at the start and end of every day to make sure that everything possible was being done to win. In the end, the company won the contract and successfully manufactured the new product. The company changed the status quo, shifting to a path that held the promise of reduced revenue volatility.

> **In sum, these leaders of industry want to optimize – not just maximize – productivity, performance, and profitability from every individual.**

Strategic delegation

The question arises as to where to find the time to focus on implementing strategy when every hour of the day is already committed to meeting current obligations. One answer is strategic delegation. Most CEOs dream of running an organization in which all managers spend the majority of their time improving the business rather than working in the business. These CEOs also wish their employees would perform at their highest potential, take personal responsibility for roles and outcomes, and be held accountable for results. In sum, these leaders of industry want to optimize – not just maximize – productivity, performance, and profitability from every individual.

Fortunately, there is a management tool to accomplish this: strategic delegation of tasks is the key to optimizing the value of each employee's output.

Without proper delegation:

- Individuals attempt to accomplish too much and get burned out or demotivated from their excessive workload.
- Opportunities to create meaningful and rewarding assignments for each staff member are overlooked.
- Quality of work suffers dramatically and deadlines are missed.
- Time management becomes a problem.
- Top performers cannot handle more high-potential activities.

Regrettably, few business schools recognize delegation as a high-priority management skill, and even fewer companies spend much time training their managers in the fine art of delegation. Consider the findings of a study conducted an economic downturn by the Institute of Corporate Productivity (i4cp)[7]. This research found that more than half (53 percent) of the 332 companies surveyed had a "somewhat high" or "high" level of concern about time-management skills, and 46 percent worried about delegation skills. However, less than half (49 percent) offer programs for time management and a mere 28 percent do so for delegation training.

It's possible that the low number of training programs on delegation is partially due to reductions in training budgets triggered by economic downturns, but there is another primary reason. Few companies truly understand the value of teaching delegation skills, of understanding why managers fail to delegate, and of learning what they can do to encourage more strategic delegation.

In any phase of the economic cycle, delegating tasks down the line is essential. In a down cycle, however, when many organizations have cut staff dramatically, knowing how to effectively delegate and maximize the efforts of everyone in the organization is especially critical. Planning enables delegation without abdication.

---

[7] The study, *The Time Management Practitioner Consensus Survey,* was conducted by i4cp in conjunction with HR.com in June 2007.

The indispensable manager

If your company culture encourages managers to feel they are indispensable, you'll get a great deal of pushback when you first broach a systems reengineering approach to enable delegation. Don't give in to it. There is only one way managers become indispensable: they make themselves so. As former French President Charles de Gaulle once said to a pompous staff member claiming to be indispensable, "The graveyards are full of indispensable men." So many folks think they are indispensable, but the world certainly keeps turning long after they are dead and gone. At some point, every employee will be gone, so don't put your company at risk from losing employees who have made themselves indispensable.

Obstacles to delegating work

Our own informal research shows that organizations that require managers to delegate are increasing their overall productivity beyond the 25 to 33 percent rate that is the average for most companies. As a result, they are beating their competition without making additional investments in people, programs, and systems. This alone would seem enough motivation for most organizations to make delegating a priority. However, even in companies where top executives take delegating seriously, something prevents managers from following through.

One of our client CEOs raised this exact concern before a recent two-day strategic planning meeting: "Why don't my managers delegate? They're limiting our growth. Changing this behavior must be a priority in our planning session."

The first step in changing this behavior is to understand what prevents managers from delegating the way they should. (I believe that it's important to understand the why's and I ask the reader to bear with me for a page or two because the dividends will be enormous.)

Four typical reasons managers resist delegating

1. They don't believe that you really want them to do it

This is largely a communication issue. Individuals need to hear on a continual basis that you expect them to manage their priorities and delegate effectively. Here are some stumbling blocks to their hearing that message:

If senior management has no tolerance for the Experience Curve that is expected in delegating a task, then delegation won't happen. In Malcolm Gladwell's book *Outliers*, he documents studies that suggest that it isn't enough to have exceptional talent. It also takes 10,000 hours of experience to completely master a skill or knowledge area. It's an important reminder that every master had to learn and master his or her trade one hour at a time, beginning with the first hour.

If the actions of senior management are inconsistent with their words, employees will pay attention only to the actions. For example, every time senior management wants quick answers to extremely detailed questions – answers that can be provided only by the person directly handling the task – then middle-level managers are not likely to delegate that task to their subordinates. Likewise, every time senior management penalizes managers for tactical missteps made by a manager's delegatee, the manager's perception that he or she should have done the work him or herself is reinforced.

If the company's focus is purely tactical and dominated by firefighting, there is probably little investment in people for the long term – something that is required if you are encouraging delegation. Because the delegation of new tasks often takes more resources and more effort – and may result in somewhat lower quantity/quality of output initially – only companies planning for the long term will be willing to pay this price to invest in the development of their staff.

2. They don't want to do it

While employees want the company and themselves to succeed, they need to know *why*, as well as *what*, we want to accomplish through delegation. They need to see the value of delegation for themselves and the company.

Fear and lack of confidence may be why managers are holding on to their "secret sauce." Some are so paranoid that they may think this requirement to delegate tasks is a secret agenda to replace them with a cheaper, younger resource. (One of our clients discovered this when instituting a policy of paying for "piece work." Many of their workers, who had figured out how to generate higher volume, were keeping their techniques secret in order to do better than their colleagues – a direct violation of the concepts of lean management.) Managers need the motivation to delegate as well as the information that will help them understand *why* delegation and personal accountability are important.

Managers believe they are not being paid to have others "do their job." Stated another way, many managers don't believe that developing others is part of their job. (Whenever our clients have promoted "top guns" to be managers, they find out that the newly promoted managers don't manage. Instead of working on the business and developing their people, they act "heroically" and do everything themselves. For example, I once worked with a vice president of marketing whose management concept included the following behavior: whenever there was a problem with Exxon, our largest client, he flew to Texas, "fixed the problem," and only talked with his Texas branch manager long after the fact. (Lacking a true marketing VP had fatal consequences.)

Managers believe it will take too long to delegate. They don't want the extra work that comes with delegating tasks. If it takes longer to delegate, why not just do the task themselves?

Some managers also want to "retain control" by doing the tasks themselves. To counter this, we teach our clients that there are other ways to exert control. For example, you can require a plan upfront and review it before granting permission to execute. Even better, by providing sustained feedback after each step in the project, you can help the delegatee quickly learn how to meet your expectations.

Managers often believe that they personally can do the best job and are further convinced that only they can do the job right. This becomes a self-fulfilling prophecy. Every time they do the job, they get even better at it, and so they remain the "best" people to do the job in the future.

Managers sometimes believe they have no one good enough to delegate tasks to. They may also believe others in the organization don't have the right attitude and aptitude. (We tested this belief with one of our clients. This management team was surprised to learn that many of their employees were demonstrating leadership and other skills in churches, scouting, and community groups. They would have been glad to take on similar challenges at work – if anyone had cared to ask them.)

Managers actually don't have anyone to delegate to because they hire only people who are less adept than they are. Why do they do this? Many managers are worried – and therefore don't want to take a chance – that someone might have the capability to do a better job than they do. When I was running larger firms, there were two reasons I would fire managers on the spot. One was when they consistently hired people less skilled than they were. (If every manager on every level hires people less qualified than himself or herself, it won't take long before you have a company of imbeciles!) The other situation was when managers told me they were "irreplaceable." I replaced them on the spot.

3. They don't know how to do it

Managers must be given training and development opportunities in the delegation skill sets. (Delegatees also need training to learn new things and get comfortable with allowing their managers to assess their progress.) Management must realize there are some costs to mandating more delegation. For example, there is a cost associated with investing time as a mentor/coach. Also, initially, results may be of lower quality and less timely than if the manager performed the task. However, if the manager is very busy, even if the delegatee takes twice as long as the manager to deliver the result – it may still get finished in half the elapsed time it would have taken the manager to get to it.

4. Managers don't have a structure/path to follow

They need a system to size, shape, and sustain progress.

Managers and delegatees need to understand the difference between delegation and abdication. The manager remains accountable for the successful outcome, and the delegatees must earn the authority to operate without close follow-up. The manager must accept and allow the delegatee to implement a task based on his or her competencies if there is to be any productivity. You might as well do the task yourself if you micromanage by not only specifying the outcomes, but also the precise way that the outcomes are accomplished. Simply stated, it's okay for the delegator to specify the final outcomes and measures but not the exact path to achieve those outcomes.

Many delegation attempts fail because the manager insists the delegatee do it his or her way or not at all. The good news is that it's many times easier to specify an outcome than the details of the action steps required to produce that outcome. If asked, of course, you can explain how you would do it.

Delegate using the model of a chief surgeon. The chief surgeon focuses on the critical aspect of the task – the critical sub-tasks – that only he or she is competent to perform and then hands over the rest of the task to the assistants in the operating and recovery rooms. This may require re-engineering the main task into a collection of sub-tasks, most of which are candidates for delegation.

Managers must learn that delegating their highest-value tasks—the A and B tasks – creates the best return. Delegating only your C and D tasks is a waste of time. Finishing those tasks delivers very low return on investment (ROI) – that's why they are C and D tasks to start with.

Strategic delegation aspects

There are four aspects of effective delegation. These include prioritizing tasks, agreeing on what sub-tasks to delegate, setting and managing expectations, and sustaining accountability and personal responsibility.

1. Prioritizing tasks

Breaking tasks into prioritized groups is a well-proven time-management process. (Prioritization is based on our friend the Pareto Principle, or the 80/20 Rule.) It is important, therefore, to prioritize tasks based on their ability to deliver value and rank tasks in order from most significant to the less significant.

Stated another way, before managers decide *what* to delegate, they must take all their potential tasks and assign them to one of the following groups:

A. A task that must be done or it will result in serious consequences.

B. A task that should be done, but has only mild consequences if left undone for a while. While important, it isn't yet urgent.

C. A task that would be nice to do but holds insignificant consequences it not done.

D. A task that could be eliminated altogether and it wouldn't make any real difference.

Among the hundreds of executive teams with whom I've worked, I have encountered several who firmly believe that delegation is a waste of time. Here's a typical comment: "I had an administrative assistant once," the executive said, "but I ended up spending more time explaining to him what to do than it was worth. It was better to just not get the work done than have to explain what I wanted." The problem was that the executive was only delegating C and D tasks – the ones he could never find the time and priority to get to. Yet, as the company grew, the bottleneck was in getting the A and B tasks done.

The key is that all managers should be working on delegating parts of their A and B tasks. There will never be a high enough ROI to sustain delegating the C and D tasks. The personal effort required to delegate C and D tasks is equal to that for the A and B tasks, albeit without the return.

> **If you focus on the most valuable 20 percent of the 20 percent of your activities – i.e., the most critical 4 percent – you can be 25 times more effective than if you performed the entire operation on your own.**

2. Agreeing on what sub-tasks to delegate

Target and take a good look at your A and B tasks. You will always be the most productive when you are focused on the things that only you can do. The question is, what sub-tasks of your A and B tasks can only you do? Referring back to the model of the chief surgeon, he or she can contribute to five times as many quality operations by restricting his or her direct involvement on the critical 20 percent of an operation. As the competence of the surgeon's interns grows, they can focus on the 20 percent of that 20 percent – i.e., the most critical 4 percent of an operation. That increases the impact the surgeon can make by another factor of five – i.e., the surgeon can be 25 times more effective than if he or she performed the entire operation.

We had a manufacturing client specializing in point-of-sale displays. He struggled to recruit sales reps. Not only was the market specialized, but also it took months for anyone new to fully master the company's complex line. We asked each sales rep, "How many hours a week do you actually spend selling?" The answer was a startling 10 hours. The other hours were spent following up on sales, filling out the paperwork for the order, making sure the plant did the job correctly, generating reports, etc. Adding another sales rep, then, would add only another ten hours a week of selling.

The company took an alternative approach, first identifying a potential delegatee who could relate to both the sales reps and the people at the plant. With training and coaching, the delegatee was able to assume responsibility for managing coordination with the plant, taking it off the plate of the sales reps. By further streamlining the order entry and reporting function, in addition to naming this assistant, each sales rep more than doubled their amount of selling time. This had the immediate effect of doubling the effectiveness of the sales force, all without having to recruit and train new sales reps! (We've used this as a standard approach to resolve other companies' bottlenecks in sales, product development, and engineering, all jobs where there is a very specialized skill set with major impact that is hard to recruit for.)

The president of a manufacturer of plastic liners and sealants also wanted his team to spend more time working on the business, rather than in it. We set a target of 20 hours per month for each executive. We had each member of the team identify five things he or she believed another team member could delegate to someone else with the total potential to free up 20 hours a month of their time. Each executive then took his or her combined list of suggested tasks, identified which tasks could truly be delegated, estimated the hours he or she spent on each, and delegated them. Within six months, each executive was spending much more time working on the business!

3. Setting and managing expectations

Make sure stakeholders of each delegated task clearly understand expectations and key measurements. Before moving to the next phase, make sure you have asked and answered the following four questions:

1. *Is it real?* (Is this a self-contained task that occurs on a regular basis?)

2. *Can the delegatee do it?* (Is the required level of competence achievable?)

3. *Can he or she win?* (In the world of competing resources, can they actually win?)

4. *Is it worth it?* (Will the payback be sufficient for both delegator and delegatee?)

4. Sustaining accountability and personal responsibility

For every task that is delegated, you must also delegate the responsibility for the quality of the work. For example, a machine operator may have been in an environment where the supervisor or quality control manager is accountable for quality. The operator runs the machine and waits for someone else to tell him or her whether the parts created in the process are acceptable. Alternatively, delegating responsibility for the quality of the worker's output to him or her shifts responsibility to someone closer to the facts on the ground and frees up time for the supervisor and the quality control manager.

The payback from delegation is much more than merely enabling managers to participate in flow-time activities like strategic planning. Delegating the

80 percent of routine work to subordinates makes managers five times more valuable. Focusing their attention on the most valuable 20 percent of the most valuable 20 percent – i.e., the absolutely most valuable 4 percent – can enable managers to become as much as 25 times more valuable. All they have to do is implement an even more aggressive delegation program, developing the competence of their subordinates to routinely handle 96 percent of their current daily tasks.

Final thoughts on implementing strategy

The secret of successful implementation is dealing with the twin challenges of focus and communications. Excellent implementation starts with a focus on the right things. The right things hold excellent answers to the following four questions:

- *Is it real?*
- *Can we do it?*
- *Can we win?*
- *Is it worth it?*

> **Picking a handful of the right things to focus on is 50 percent of success. The other 50 percent comes from ongoing, effective communications.**

Picking a handful of the right things to focus on is 50 percent of success. The other 50 percent comes from ongoing, effective communications. Regular, well-facilitated meetings allow stakeholders to share lessons learned, let the company utilize their wisdom, and keep everybody on the same page with the same expectations.

The challenges of focus and communication will never be "solved."

They are ongoing challenges that require a continuous process and constant vigilance.

The next chapter deals with "people chemistry," ultimately the most important component in the chemistry of growth. That's because leather-bound documents and PowerPoint slides don't implement strategy – people do.

CHAPTER SUMMARY
The Chemistry of Implementation

What are the major concepts in this chapter?

- Communication of *what*, *why*, and *how* is required for a successful implementation of your strategy.
- Implementation always impacts and involves multiple people who need to periodically meet and realign their understanding, expectations, and responsibilities.
- Strategic delegation can free up the resources to focus on implementing strategy.
- Success depends on the personal accountability of individuals who understand *what's* strategically important to do, understand *why* it's valuable to the company and themselves to do it, know *how* to actually do it, and have a system to keep them on track.
- The ongoing challenge is to keep everyone focused on the right tasks while repeatedly communicating by connecting the dots between today's action steps and the company's visualized future.

Why are these major concepts important?

- Failure to implement wastes resources while breeding frustration and cynicism.
- Failure to implement leaves control of the future to chance.

How can you apply these major concepts?

- Continuously communicate, sharing with everyone *what* you are looking to accomplish this year, and *why* those accomplishments are strategic, and connecting the dots between today's actions and your envisioned future so everyone involved with implementation understands.
- Form working teams that meet on an ongoing basis to assess progress to date, reach agreement on the next steps, settle on

who is personally accountable for the next steps, and decide what the next set of tactical actions are.

- Make sure there is a single, named individual personally accountable for each strategic goal, key result measure, and each action step.
- Re-engineer your processes to enable strategic delegation and use it to increase your strategic capacity.
- Work with your middle managers to determine *how* to achieve those objectives.

Want more? Download a FREE workbook at myrna.com/books

Like this book? Please leave a review at Amazon.com!

Chapter 10
People Chemistry: Engaged, Empowered, and Accountable

"People never learn anything by being told, they have to find out for themselves."
                                                         Paulo Coelho

"If you want to build a ship, don't drum up the men to gather wood, divide the work and give orders. Instead, teach them to yearn for the vast and endless sea."
                                                         Antoine de Saint-Exupery

It all started simply enough. I was facilitating a strategic planning review meeting for a family business, Wicket Worldwide. The usual agenda for the day included a meeting with the executive management team in the morning, with the middle managers joining us in the afternoon. The major topic of discussion with the executive managers was how to best engage the middle managers in the strategic planning process. The middle managers had provided feedback from previous meetings that they really couldn't afford the time the planning meetings took. It had been obvious during the previous meetings that too many participants were accepting cell phone calls, texting, and reading and responding to e-mails. They were not fully listening and participating. This behavior confused me and the executive managers, since for years the middle managers had been asking for more participation and more say in the decisions that affected their lives and jobs. Participation in the planning meetings appeared to be an ideal way to engage them. The owners felt as frustrated as a minister who has been preaching the benefits of a virtuous life with no apparent daily impact on the congregation.

This time around, the executive team asked me to meet alone with the middle managers in the afternoon, in hopes that I could get a clearer sense of how to structure the afternoon planning meetings to optimize their value and people's participation. Without their managers in attendance, the middle managers opened up in the afternoon session. Although there was much shared frustration, everyone on the middle-management team conveyed an obvious and strong passion for the success of Wicket Worldwide and the Wicket family, which had founded and still ran the business. The team seemed eager to contribute to both the success of the company and the smooth transition to the next generation of family management. The situation seemed favorable – at least on the surface. However, during our discussions, the root causes of middle management's dissatisfaction became apparent. It wasn't the structure of the planning meetings inhibiting the managers; it was the company's policies and procedures that stymied their engagement. Simply stated, the system made it impossible to empower them.

Wicket's hands-on management paradigm, embedded in their policies and procedures, created a company-wide dependence on the timely availability of a supervising manager to provide an answer and make a decision for just about any meaningful action to proceed. Everyone in the organization was constantly hamstrung by being without the authority to do more than wait for approval before acting. The middle managers couldn't afford to be involved in any task like strategic planning that required them to be incommunicado, since operations would literally grind to a halt if they couldn't be reached. Enabling Wicket's managers to take on any tasks – including strategic planning—that required them to be unavailable for their regular job-related activities for extended periods of time (be it minutes, hours, or days) would require the reengineering of the systems they were personally baked into.

Over the next two years, Wicket identified the opportunities at every management level to reengineer how to apply experience and expertise without requiring someone's real-time approval. By phasing out the requirement for a manager's real-time presence, they removed the bottlenecks created whenever that manager wasn't available to respond for any reason— sickness, travel, vacation, critical projects, or meetings. Not only did this empower the middle managers to be actively engaged in strategy, the changes in policies and procedures ended up empowering all employees.

Chapter focus

This chapter discusses how to implement policies and procedures that empower employees, increase capacity through delegation, and enhance mutual trust.

Fully empowered employees

Empowered employees are the final ingredient in a successful strategy. The executive leadership team has mixed all the strategic elements together to create the best strategy and plan. They have laid out the systems for effective implementation. Now they execute through the daily actions of an engaged, empowered, and accountable workforce.

*The Oxford Dictionary definition of the verb **empower** is:*
[with object and infinitive] give (someone) the authority or power to do something
[with object] make (someone) stronger and more confident, especially in controlling their life and claiming their rights.

An employee requires knowledge of four things to be fully empowered in their job:

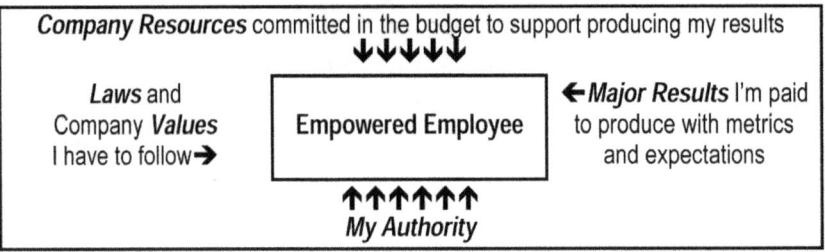

Clarity about the results they are paid to produce and how they are measured. The job description and standards of performance should clearly establish a small set of key expected results and how they will be measured. This focuses the employee on a small set of results rather than the long list of activities necessary to achieve those results.

Resources consistent with those desired results. The budget is the company's commitment of resources as well as a tool for organizational control and limits. Ideally there is a negotiation between the employee and the company during budgeting. The employee commits to specific, measurable results and the company commits to the resources the employee needs to deliver those results.

Constraints on pursuing those results established by laws and the company's values. Company values articulate the level of ethics and integrity expected from all employees

Authority to act independently when pursuing those results. Empowered employees can rightfully assume they have the authority necessary to fulfill their jobs, but for a small list of exceptions. These exceptions are individually set, based on a particular employee's demonstrated judgment and the overall risk of a decision to the organization. Typically the risks deal with making long-term commitments (such as hiring, leases, and committing cash resources) by limiting spending and expense account authority.

True empowerment

True empowerment can't be granted; it has to come from within the heart and soul of the employee. The organization can set expectations and limits as a first step, but in many cases it takes careful coaching, counseling and nurturing to spark that spirit.

On the other hand, company culture, as well as its policies and procedures, can make it impossible to empower employees.

Endothermic policies and procedures

Chemical reactions are endothermic (absorb heat) or exothermic (exude heat). If the people you depend on for implementation aren't engaged, empowered, and accountable, they will suck all the energy out of your strategy. It is the responsibility of executive leadership to make sure employees are empowered to proactively support the company's strategy. Empowered employees add energy to your strategy.

Engagement and empowerment

"This year, let's see if we can implement differently." Jude, the general manager of Alpha's U.S. division, challenged his colleagues at the planning meeting. "Last year it seems that most of our objectives were implemented by the senior leadership team. How can we fully engage and empower the workforce?" Before we moved on, I asked each team member to describe the behavior of an engaged employee. (I commonly ask team members to describe their personal interpretation of words like "accountable," "teamwork," and "engagement.") The responses provided us with nuanced information about *what* engagement looked like to Alpha's team. This was Alpha's jumping-off point for identifying *how* to achieve that strategic goal.

Their responses when asked to define "engaged, empowered employees" were as follows:

- They act within the company's core values and espouse them.
- They are observably connected – you can see that they are committed, prioritizing their daily actions based on what's best for the company.
- They contribute, personally creating value.
- They deliver results – even if they initially have to be pulled along by the ear.
- They figure out the missing pieces of any task on their own.
- They have an ownership mentality.
- They have the expectation of participating, asking "How can I help?"
- They help shape company processes, including strategic planning.
- They live, communicate, and advocate the company's strategic plan to others.
- They understand that they make a difference – that they are important.
- They understand the company's strategic direction, strategy, and what it means to them.

> **Step one of getting the engagement of empowered employees is to actually empower them.**

Walk the talk

This is the behavior executive managers expect from their employees. Employees, on the other hand, expect all the talk about engagement and empowerment to be backed up with specific management behaviors. It isn't enough to tell people you want them to take responsibility and be empowered; management needs to *walk the talk* by engineering company policies and procedures to enable that empowerment. The team's empowered employee responses included the following "walk the talk" items:

- They expect *assistance* in gaining the competence to exercise their responsibilities.
- They expect the *authority* to control the routine aspects of their jobs. (The more aspects of their jobs employees can control, the more empowered they feel.)
- They expect the *respect* demonstrated by having their input solicited and considered before decisions that affect them are made.
- They expect *timely responses* when they require information or approval to execute their responsibilities.
- They expect, request, and provide *feedback*.

Step one of getting the engagement of empowered employees is to actually empower them. It's a simple concept, but one that's all too easy to mishandle.

Where to start

Personal accountability starts with making the employee responsible for the most important aspect of their employment – their annual review. What goes through the mind of any employee when they hear their manager say "I'm sorry, but we'll have to delay your performance review, something important came up." Something important came up? What am I, the employee is thinking, chopped liver?

The challenge with performance reviews is that the monkey is on the back of the manager. Typically he has several direct reports. He has to fill out multi-page forms, schedule meetings, and handle all the other aspects of a big company formal review. What I've observed in practice is that annual reviews seldom get done annually to the frustration of employees, managers, and senior executives alike. Consider turning the process on its head.

- Make each employee responsible for one and only one performance review – their own.

- Have each employee fill out the major part of the paperwork themselves, forwarding the completed documentation to their manager.
- Have each employee schedule the performance review meeting with their manager.
- In the performance review meeting, have the employee review their past performance while the employee's manager shares his or her assessment of the employee. Together they review the current job description and agree on changes to the expected results and metrics, levels of authority, and changes in resources the company will commit.
- In the performance review meeting, have each employee discuss their long-term goals within the company, and together with their manager, agree on a development plan for the coming year.

The empowered have authority in balance with responsibility

With a simple ten-second W.A.S.T.E. coaching technique, managers can be a proactive force in facilitating their direct reports' progress to higher levels of authority. (The acronym stands for Wait. Ask. Suggest. Tell. Empowered in the Authority Table™.) Before telling your employee what action to take, pause and ask them one simple yet powerful question. If the employee is at:

Level 1 – *Wait until told what to do* – ask them:

"What do you see that you think requires action?" When they can consistently recognize the need for action, they will automatically move to Level 2.

Level 2 – *Ask for direction* – ask them:

"What actions do you think we could take?" When they consistently come up with feasible actions, move them to Level 3. Tell them you expect suggested actions.

Authority Table™

Levels of authority for each responsibility each level of **authority** derives from demonstrated, or assumed, **competence**	1 **Wait** until told what to do	2 **Ask** for direction	3 **Suggest** action	4 **Tell** after acting	5 **Empowered** to act independently
Responsibility 1				√	
Responsibility 2				√	
Responsibility 3			√		
Responsibility 4			√		
Responsibility 5		√			

√ Identifies minimum authority/competence required to fulfill each responsibility

Level 3 – *Suggest* action – ask them:

"What action would you recommend?" When they consistently recommend a viable action, move them to Level 4. Tell them you expect them to act on their best judgment and have them review their actions with you at the first opportunity.

Level 4 – *Tell after acting* – ask them:

"Are you learning anything from reviewing your actions with me?" When the answer is no, move them to Level 5. Tell them they are fully empowered to act independently for those responsibilities.

Level 5 – *Empowered* – remind them that "with greater authority comes greater accountability." They do not have the authority to do stupid things.

The greater the number of daily decisions that don't require prior approval from a senior manager, the smoother and faster a company functions. Strategic goals are strategic because they change the status quo. Implementing and sustaining *W.A.S.T.E.* coaching is a real status quo changer. (*W*ait. *A*sk. *S*uggest. *T*ell. *E*mpowered is a powerful technique in order to not "waste" valuable human capital.)

This coaching approach also works in reverse. For example, if an employee starts making poor decisions, you need to move them down a level of authority. "Until further notice Bruce, you need to check with me first before meeting with the regulators." You can't reduce an employee's authority below the level required for that job without impacting smooth operations. You and the employee need to agree on an action plan to resolve the problem, typically in less than 90 days. The resolution can be as simple as having the employee update their knowledge of current regulations at an industry workshop. Or, it can be as painful as replacing the employee with someone with the competence to handle compliance with ever-more-complex regulations. Assuming the employee has the capacity to regain it, losing authority hurts and is an effective motivator.

An ideal time to review levels of authority is during an employee's annual review. As a company grows and evolves, the competencies required by the current position will change. Each employee should be encouraged to identify the next position they are shooting for. Based on the position the employee and manager have targeted, you need to:

- Identify gaps between what's needed and the employee's current experience.
- Align the gap with employee's personal goals.
- Make an explicit, mutual agreement that the employee can fill the gap.
- Discuss and agree on gap-filling strategies.
- Pay close attention to progress in this area.

Problems traditionally occur because the manager or employee will *assume* a level of authority that the employee can't or won't handle. You can prevent a host of future problems if you establish the appropriate levels of authority *before* the employee or company gets in trouble.

Many companies pride themselves on fostering a "hands-on" management style like the one used at Wicket Worldwide. Individual managers, from the CEO down, actively participate in the daily operation of the business. Although their real-time participation guarantees that their judgment and expertise gets applied to even the most mundane operational decisions, it is a double-edged sword. When managers have to approve everything, there is no way the rest of the team can be truly empowered, feel valued, or be trusted. For example, how empowered can employees of Wicket feel when they have to justify the need for purchasing something as minor as a replacement printer cartridge? Management shouldn't have been bewildered that its employees stopped caring after such a printer-cartridge policy was instituted.

Realizing the benefits of hands-on management doesn't automatically require direct control of all decisions. There are better approaches to providing oversight and control than forcing employees to obtain permission before acting. For routine decisions with low risk, control and accountability can be exerted by a manager through regular review of their subordinates' decisions – i.e. raising their authority to Level 4, "Tell after acting."

Wicket, for example, revised its policy on business expenditures to provide every employee with a dollar amount that he or she was authorized to spend without prior approval. Along with that policy, a system was put in place to hold employees accountable for those decisions by reviewing them daily, weekly, or monthly, as appropriate. The dollar amounts were set by considering both the employees' demonstrated judgment and the needs of their positions. For example, any employee could feel free to buy a soda or cup of coffee for a customer. A branch office manager could purchase printer cartridges or a box of pens when needed, no questions asked.

Over time, you can align each employee's daily work with company values and goals by making every employee's decisions transparent and then holding them personally accountable for those decisions.

Utilize your management team effectively

In my experience, it isn't useful to frame your staffing issues around "good" employees and "bad" employees. A more useful framework is to think of employees as either being in the right job for them or in the wrong job. As we've learned, typically 20 percent of your workers are in the perfect jobs for them— and 20 percent are in the worst job for them. The elements that create that fit include how passionate they are about their jobs, how competent they are in their jobs, and how well the requirements of the jobs align with the employees' personal needs. (See the expanded discussion on this in Chapter 7.)

The Platinum Paradigm™

Employee performance will be platinum, gold, silver, bronze, tin, or lead based on how well the individual's **passion**, **competence**, and personal **alignment** matches their current job

%	Description	Tier
4%	your super performers, self-actualized (the 20% of the 20%)	*platinum*
16%	your great performers – lavish rewards and attention on these folks	*gold*
30%	the core of steady performing folks	*silver*
30%	folks not quite with it - striving to improve or drifting lower	*bronze*
16%	folks just getting by - drifting lower or struggling to improve	*tin*
4%	folks trapped in a negative spiral, frustrating everyone	*lead*

Transition folks who are trapped in the wrong job for them - the organization's lead weights. Eliminating lead's negative energy motivates the tin and bronze to enhance their fit. Alchemists wasted lives trying to transmute lead into gold – be a manager not an alchemist.

Along with the short-term alignment, there needs to be a commitment to reengineering policies and/or procedures so that a lower-level associate could take real-time action more often— ideally 80 percent or more. Doing this at Wicket increased productivity, improved turnaround time and made it practical for a manager to work on activities like planning that require large blocks of uninterrupted time. Typically, 20 percent of a manager's decisions produce 80 percent of the impact (the Pareto Principle). Reengineering systems to delegate the lower-impact 80 percent of decisions allows managers to focus more brain power on the most important ones. It also increases the likelihood that the manager would be able to make decisions on the remaining 20 percent in a timely manner.

Strategic delegation

If you don't delegate you can't be promoted and the company can't grow. The ultimate fate for managers who believe they can become irreplaceable by not delegating is to find themselves replaced. The successful CEO will not allow an irreplaceable manager to prevent his company from growing. Further, delegation frees up the resources required to implement strategy. (Chapter 9 outlines approaches to effective delegation.)

Developing trust is key

The hands-on management paradigm can be a vehicle for building trust or it can be a trust inhibitor. When hands-on implementation focuses on control and negative feedback, people are reluctant to discuss issues with their managers in direct attendance. When a manager uses negative feedback as a club, it's no surprise that their subordinates keep their thoughts to themselves. People stop talking to managers who respond defensively to issues raised rather than listen and work to understand underlying issues. In discussing weaknesses, it's all too easy to gloss over negative input as "complaining," instead of viewing it as a productive way of identifying areas for improvement.

Trust acts like a lubricant in the running of an organization. When you deal with problems from a position of trust, you don't waste time placing blame or being defensive. When working on multi-team projects in a trusting atmosphere, you don't have to invest as much time in checking up on people. Different organizational levels of management feel free to raise issues without fear, thus eliminating many problems before they occur. Remember that in order to trust individuals; you must satisfy yourself that they possess three key traits:

1. *Character*. Do they tell the truth? Do they follow through? If they can't answer a question or don't know the answer, do they make up a story?

2. *Competence*. Do they know how to do the job? Do they have the skills and common sense consistent with their responsibilities/authority?

3. **Caring.** Do they care about *your* goals, needs, and objectives? Are their agendas aligned with yours? People don't care how much you know until they know how much you care.

Social engagement builds trust. Over the past 30 years, I've had the opportunity to work not only with for-profit companies but also with various nonprofits dedicated to improving opportunities for specific minority groups. One of the most effective ways to break down stereotypes is a process called "social engagement" – essentially, spending time working with members of the stereotyped group. If executives don't interact with nonexecutives, if managers don't interact with subordinates, they can easily be seen as the stereotypical uncaring, untrustworthy ogres.

> **Employees know they are respected when their input is solicited, understood, and considered before decisions that affect them are made.**

Respect – R E S P E C T

Empowered employees feel respected. Employees know they are respected when their input is solicited, understood, and considered *before* decisions that affect them are made. Planning meetings are one tool for implementing respect, as is "management by walking around." Set a policy that when managers draft new policies, they must chat with those affected *before* finalizing and publishing the operating version.

Another way to let your employees know they are respected is to offer a timely response to e-mails and telephone calls. At Wicket, managers commented about how hard it was to trust the purchasing manager. "He doesn't care about me or what I need for my job. His office door is always closed, and he doesn't answer his phone or respond to e-mail. I can't get the simplest answer from him." When pushed, the manager acknowledged that in response he didn't always worry about responding to the purchasing manager's requests. "He doesn't respect me, why should I respect him?"

Asking rather than telling reinforces empowerment. Most employees care deeply about their company. When managers *ask* for their help, rather than *telling* employees to do something, it let employees say yes and demonstrate that caring.

Show respect by communicating an expectation that "complaints" will be solicited and listened to without placing blame or being defensive. Coach your managers to focus their questions on achieving clarification and understanding. Every manager's behavior should communicate that there is no reason to fear being punished or belittled for raising an issue. Make a point of listening, paraphrasing for clarity, and truly considering each employee's input.

Empowering strategy

Designing anything – whether it's a new process, product, or strategic plan – is inherently one of making complex trade-offs. Consider the process of designing a new product. Customers want you to include every possible feature, they want the new product available yesterday, and they prefer it to be free. Every design is the result of balancing the considerations of quality, quantity, timeliness, and cost. In the design process, an individual or design team brings up each issue in turn. One by one, each new issue is put into play. At a magic moment, every relevant issue is clearly in each participant's mind and the design team starts to make trade-offs among them.

Psychologists talk about entering a *state of flow* when all the issues are clear in your mind. It takes an individual 15 to 20 minutes to achieve such a state of flow. It takes even more time for a team to achieve flow. It takes just one interruption to drop someone out of flow. All it takes is responding to a telephone call, reading an e-mail, or mentally drifting off to consider an issue unrelated to the matter at hand. The greater the number of issues to be balanced in the design process and the higher the risk associated with your decisions, the more time you need to focus your attention. We have developed an informal metric we call the *focus quotient*. It is the number of hours an individual can focus and be unavailable for short-term operational decisions before there is a significant negative impact on the company's performance.

Empowering managers to take on tasks like strategic planning will require them to be in an extended state of flow and unavailable for their regular job-related activities for extended periods of time (be it minutes, hours, or days.) This requires a change in the status quo by reengineering any system they are personally baked into. If your managers have *focus quotients* of minutes rather than hours, they are unavailable to invest the time optimal for strategic planning.

Have your managers talk one-on-one with each of their people about the best role for each employee's support of the company strategy, based on the employee's current mix of passion, competence, and alignment. Clarify expectations and what actions are required and expected in both the short and long terms. Ask which of their manager's planning-related "micromanagement" tasks they could assume and determine how that transition can take place. Identify managers with low focus quotients but a passion for participation in flow-time activities like planning or whose input is considered essential. Put a priority on reengineering their responsibilities to enable them spend more time working on the business rather than in the business.

Help employees gain the competence required to earn the empowering *authority* they seek. Reengineer processes to support that empowerment by transitioning hands-on management to hands-on coaching. Set and maintain an expectation for a timely response to every request for information, review, or decision.

Reengineer the policies that undermine empowerment. Set a reasonable level of authority for unapproved purchases that don't need higher-level approval, such as enough to cover the typical no-brainer decisions managers make every month. Match the new authority with an ongoing review process that holds them accountable for their decisions. Don't forget to tell your employees that you *expect* their engagement.

Here's the hardest step: work with your managers to recognize behavior inconsistent with exhibiting the empowerment behaviors of respect, authority, assistance, and timely response.

Ben Franklin attended Sunday service just about every week of his life. He was bemused that ministers gave sermons telling the congregation to live a virtuous life while assuming everyone could figure out how to do that on their own. Among Franklin's many accomplishments was a specific thirteen-point system for living a virtuous life. It isn't enough to tell people they can't access their iPhones during a long meeting. It isn't enough to tell employees they need to be engaged and empowered. And, it isn't enough to tell your managers they can't allow themselves to become indispensible.

You must move beyond the talk and reengineer the status quo policies, procedures, and expectations that are preventing these virtuous behaviors around engagement and empowerment. Like Franklin, you must coach your people on exactly how to walk the talk – and be sure to walk that talk yourself.

Let's move on to the last chapter, where we sum up the chemistry of growth.

CHAPTER SUMMARY

People Chemistry: Engaged, Empowered, and Accountable

What are the major concepts in this chapter?

- Delegation is a key process for increasing the capacity of the organization as well as empowerment and accountability.
- Employees want to succeed. To be truly engaged, they need to know *why*, as well as *what*, we want to accomplish.
- Hands-on management can smother personal accountability and empowerment.
- Trust is an organization's lubricant. When everyone trusts each other's *character*, *competence*, and *caring*, things run smoothly.

Why are these major concepts important?

- When employees know *what* the company wants from them and believe in the *why*, they will, like salmon swimming upstream, push through any and all obstacles to achieve.

How can you apply these major concepts?

- Establish policies that empower employees with appropriate authority while holding them personally accountable for the outcomes of their work.
- Inculcate the behaviors that build and sustain trust and respect.
- Make every employee responsible for their career, starting with their annual performance review.
- Utilize strategic delegation to foster ownership, empowerment, and personal accountability.

Want more? Download a FREE workbook at myrna.com/books

Chapter 11
Conclusion: The Chemistry of Breakthrough Leadership

"When you reach for the stars you may not quite get one, but you won't come up with a handful of mud either."

Leo Burnett

"The greater danger for most of us lies not in setting our aim too high and falling short, but in setting our aim too low and achieving our mark."

Michelangelo

During our annual strategic planning meeting, I asked Jeff, the CEO of one of our longest-running strategic planning clients, how they fared during the worst of the last major economic downturn. "Well, John, industry demand dropped over 30 percent, some big players failed or were purchased, and every customer demanded a discount."

"But how did *you* do?" I asked. "Not so bad," Jeff replied. "We upgraded our production facility as planned, continued to invest in expanding our product line, and remained profitable – and we are growing again and gaining market share."

Sandy, the newly hired human resources director, chimed in. "How exactly were we able to manage the tough times and continue to support investment in the future? My previous employer wasn't so lucky."

"Luck didn't have anything to do with it!" exclaimed Mike, the head of production. "In the nine years I've been here, we've totally changed things for the better." He rattled off a few of those strategic changes:

- "We developed flexible staffing strategies with cross-training, added a third shift, and optimized a full-time / temporary worker mix based on real-time demand. This enabled us to quickly and profitably handle both surges and dips in demand."
- "We developed sophisticated bidding strategies that enabled us to increase the percentage of bids won and managed for profit."
- "We diversified our customer base, minimizing the impact of having our largest customer go out of business."
- "We put reporting in place and trained our managers and supervisors to understand and use those reports to make real-time adjustments."
- "We upgraded our management systems, enabling more efficient production scheduling and capturing true costs."

> **Year after year, they had identified and implemented strategic goals that literally changed their status quo.**

Over the past decade, their executive leadership team had set a shared vision of the future that reached for the stars. Year after year, they had identified

CONCLUSION: THE CHEMISTRY OF BREAKTHROUGH LEADERSHIP

and implemented strategic goals that literally changed their status quo. They had mastered the chemistry of growth, mixing together elements of focus, communications, risk, diversification, empowerment, and leadership in just the right proportions at just the right time to grow into the company they all visualized.

Jeff summed it up: "I guess the breakthrough for us has been the discipline imposed by our commitment to the strategic planning process."

Chapter focus

Take control of your destiny by creating your future.

The breakthrough

I went to graduate school in Bozeman, Montana. When I wasn't in the computer center doing programming, I was at Bridger Bowl, skiing. There were skiers who would fall every ten yards, even when moving slowly down the beginner or "bunny" slope. Then there were skiers who could navigate the most difficult black diamond runs at blinding speed, handling moguls, recovering with quick tucks, never even stumbling. The difference in their performance wasn't due to how fast they were moving. The difference was due to their skiing only as fast as their ability to remain in control. With training, coaching, and hours spent on the slopes, I eventually was able to ski faster and handle more advanced slopes.

In the same way, high-growth companies reap the rewards that come from investing in improving their processes, forecasting ability, control systems and employee competence. No company grows by cutting expenses or staying on the "bunny slope." Companies grow by improving their productivity, business acumen, and overall ability to manage risk. Strategic planning is the essential catalyst for that type of controlled growth. Remember, every organization's mission is to create and grow value for its stakeholders. (Stakeholders being customers, employees, owners, vendors, communities, et al. Value being measured in multiple ways, not only financial.)

Ad astra per aspera – to the stars through difficulty

"I didn't know how we were going to get here six years ago, but we did!" Susan, CEO of a telecom services firm, was sharing her company's results with her CEO peer group. "Six years ago, when we started our strategic planning process, my executive leadership team painted a picture of where we wanted to be within five years. I was skeptical, as they were more ambitious than I expected them to be, or frankly than I thought we could accomplish. But we sustained the strategic planning process, adjusting our short-term tactics while remaining focused on the long-term. And, like magic, we did it."

> **Aim for the stars and enjoy the journey along the way.**

Over the years I've heard the same success story repeated over and over again. You too can take control of your destiny when you:

- Create a shared strategy for *what* you want the future to look like.
- Understand, communicate, and embrace *why* this future creates value for all your stakeholders.
- Live your life by knowing *how* today's actions remain consistent with advancing that strategy.

Aim for the stars and enjoy the journey along the way.

CHAPTER SUMMARY

Conclusion: The Chemistry of Breakthrough Leadership

What are the major concepts in this chapter?

- Take control of your destiny by creating your future.

Why are these major concepts important?

- We all should be good stewards and create the most value from the resources under our management.

How can you apply these major concepts?

- Develop and sustain a healthy executive leadership team.
- Deploy that team to create, document, and communicate a shared strategic vision.
- Engage, empower and hold every employee accountable for its implementation.
- Prioritize today's actions based on how well they support your strategic vision.
- Utilize an ongoing, facilitated strategic planning process that turns your vision into reality.

Want more? Download a FREE workbook at myrna.com/books

Like this book? Please leave a review at Amazon.com!

Definitions

Accountable Person: A *single named individual* who can account for *where we are* with regards to a key result measure, *why we're there*, and *what we're doing* about it – i.e. what are the next 90 days of action steps.

Action Plan: An organization of personal commitments that serves as a vehicle for causing a strategic goal to become a reality. It is comprised of:

- A **Strategic Goal** statement – a pithy one-liner that captures the spirit of the required change to the status quo.
- A **Champion, Co-Champions** – persons who are accountable for shepherding the goal to completion.
- A list of **Key Result Measures (KRM)** – comprehensive, specific set of outcomes that define completion for the team.
- An **Accountable Person** for each key result measure – the single, named individual accountable for the KRM.
- A set of 90-day **Action Steps** – specific actions to be finished in the next days and weeks that create results.

Champion: A named individual who represents the planning team's best mix of passion and competence, for shepherding a *Strategic Goal* over the next 12 to 18 months. This champion decides *how* the goal gets done while remaining accountable for *what* gets done through delivery of the team-set *key result measures* and operating through plans that are written, understood, reviewed, and approved. An individual is the champion of one and only one goal. They and their co-champions are the forward wedge, personally guaranteeing that their goal is moving forward and will be completed as rapidly and completely as possible. They clear the way, garnering support and resources. They know the current state of progress on their goal at all times. They build and maintain corporate awareness and support. They represent the consensus and commitment of the entire planning team.

Co-champion(s): The team members accountable for the key result measures under the goal.

Customer: Someone who **has bought from you more than once** in the recent past – typically over the last one to two years. The customer can be recognized as the one with the open wallet. (There may be many end users that your products must attract and service but if you don't also meet the needs of the customer you will never make a sale!)

End Users: The individuals who **ultimately use your product**. If your product does not meet the needs of the ultimate users there will be no motivation on the part of your customer to buy it. (For example, end users of Dove soap ask Wal-Mart, Unilever's potential customer, to carry the product.)

Market: A **collection of prospects** you have an effective way to **communicate** with, that have **common needs** that can be met by products your product group can develop, your sales team can deliver, and your customer services group **can support**, that can generate **enough revenue** to be relevant at your current size. Markets can be defined by any criteria that groups your prospects – such as application, function, geography, job title, or industry.

Mission: Your realm of activity over the next three to five years to fulfill your vision. It is an affirmation of:

- *What do you want to be?* (Usually some statement of leadership)
- *What customers do you want to do it for?* (Usually a statement of geographic scope, industry, targeted customer profile)
- *Why do you do it?* (Usually to create value for your customers, employees, and owners along with a "softer" thought like aid the environment, save lives, have fun – if it's true)
- *How do you want to do it?* (Usually some combination of develop, manufacture, supply, or market specific services or products)

Product: The manifestation of the *value you create* for your customer. The "thing" they pay you for. Sometimes it is a physical object like cables, screws, or disks, and sometimes it is an intangible, such as advice.

Sale: A *one-time event* when money changes hands. The first sale typically costs more than the profit it generates. Typically you can only make a profit once there are multiple sales to the same organization – i.e., sales don't build a business, customers build a business.

Vision: The embodiment of your organization's internal gyroscope consisting of your *core purpose*, *core values* and a 10 to 30-year *goal*.

Resources

Isaac Newton, English physicist, mathematician, astronomer, alchemist, inventor and natural philosopher, said it best.

> "If I have seen further it is only by standing on the shoulders of giants."
>
> *Isaac Newton*

Myrna Associates' "Big Hairy Audacious Goal" is to motivate every organization to experience the power of strategic management. For over thirty years, we have relentlessly pursued the development of the world's most effective strategic planning process. Along the way, we have been enriched by the insights of innumerable senior strategic planning teams. An integral element of our process is capturing and refining those insights. You can tap into this pool of insights through our monthly newsletter, regular blogs, monthly webinars, published articles, how-to books, and tweets.

Please find all these resources on our website: http://www.myrna.com/resources:

- A free 16-page report, "Are You Ready for Strategic Planning?"
- Access to our newsletters.
- LinkedIn postings.
- Links to related books and webinars.

Acknowledgements

This book reflects the insights gained from the hundreds of senior executives I've worked with during strategic planning meetings over many years. Their suggestions for new and better approaches, as well as their tendency to force me to think through *why* a process worked as well as it did were a constant inspiration. Every process discussed in this book has been enhanced and field-proven in the crucible of those thousands of hours of creating and implementing strategic plans.

This book wouldn't have happened without Ken Lizotte of the emerson counsulting group. He was the catalyst, pushing and guiding me to the finish line, and instrumental in matching me with the ideal publisher.

James Bergsten, Maria Birkhead, Daniel Dyer, Gretchen Farb, Alex Hoffer, Alex Kronemer, and Robert Posten's careful review of an early version of the manuscript helped enhance the clarity and flow of the book. Special thanks to Maria Birkhead, Mary Myrna, and Brett Wallace for their review of especially difficult chapters.

Gabriel Goldberg, Joseph Mancuso, Lee B. Salz, and Tom Searcy shared their personal experiences in and insights about the process of writing and publishing a book of this scale.

Special thanks to Maria Birkhead, Senior Facilitator at Myrna Associates, for over two decades we've shared facilitation insights. Working with her has been a real joy.

Thanks to Daniel Dyer, founder of STSC, who made me part of STSC's first strategic planning team in 1976. This was one of the defining moments of my life.

The excellent layout of this book is the work of Kevin O'Connor. I especially appreciate his patience as we fine tuned the final version of the text.

Thanks to Cindy Murphy and Elena Petricone for the final touches.

And then there is Kate Victory Hannisian, my editor at emerson consulting group. What more can I say about how my written voice has been enhanced through her years of thoughtful editing?

Many thanks to Jennifer Baarson, my Marketing Manager for the myriad of ways she made this a better book.

About the Author

John W. Myrna is cofounder of Myrna Associates Inc., a company that helps organizations thrive by facilitating new strategic plans, formulating actionable tactics, and evaluating workforce performance against those plans. His team helps clients create and grow value by turning their vision into reality using proprietary methodologies as part of intense, two-day off-site sessions. Along with a passion for teaching and his broad business experience and knowledge, John has a gift for bringing out the best in companies and their management teams. *The Chemistry of Growth* is based on John's experiences in running and turning around mid-sized companies, and his 30 years facilitating effective strategic planning for hundreds of organizations. In addition to regularly publishing articles and speaking to business audiences, John has contributed chapters on strategic business planning and implementation to *The Business Expert Guide to Small Business Success*, and is the author of four previous books. He also coaches CEOs one-to-one.

Contact John via e-mail at tcog@myrna.com, connect with johnwmyrna on LinkedIn, or visit his website at myrna.com.

Index

10,000 hours of experience 60, 137

A

Absentee, The (meeting archetype) 17

accountability 46, 117, 131, 159

accountable person 46, 173

accuracy (more important than precision) 44

ad astra per aspera (to the stars through difficulty) 170

ancient Greeks (believed gods on Mount Olympus controlled dice) 50

archetypes, meeting behavior 17

Aristotle
  paraphrase 90
  quote 83

Atkins, P. W., quote 7

attitude and aptitude 103

Authority Table™, The (illustration) 106

B

Bell, Alexander Graham, quote 99

Berra, Yogi quote 33

Big Hairy Audacious Goal 43, 47

branding 44, 95

Buffet, Warren, quote 58

Built to Last 43

Burnett, Leo, quote 167

C

C-level executives 8, 10

catalyst, definition 34

CEO
  as facilitator 23, 26
  internal vs. external focus 57
  key member of planning team 38

number one challenge of   10

plan ownership by   50

replacing a loyal employee   60

responsibilities that can't be delegated   38

role in strategic planning meetings   32

CFO

   model for accountability   46

   number one challenge of   10

   strategy of adding CFO role   32, 56

champion, definition   173

Chief Executive Omniscience (meeting archetype)   17

Christensen, Clayton M., author of *The Innovator's Dilemma*   61

co-champion, definition   174

Coelho, Paulo, quote   149

Collins, Jim, author of *Built to Last*   43

communications

   communication and focus   39

   half of implementation   144

   need to "connect the dots"   133

   strategic plan as a tool   20

Confucius, quote   102

Consultant, The (meeting archetype)   18

consultants, utilizing   37, 50

core purpose, beyond "making money"   42, 175

cost of quality   115, 122

critical mass

   definition   12

   example of Acme's single customer focus   71

   need for multiple customers/transactions   88

   reaching breakeven   89

   underpins product/market strategy   84

culture

   definition of corporate culture   60

   impact on employee actions   128

customer, definition   174

D

de Gaulle, Charles, quote

delegation

   example of company executives freeing up 20 hours/month   142

   example of point-of-sale display company   142

   strategic (how to)   135, 140, 161

INDEX

diversification
    example of specialty manufacturing 86
    The Expansion Matrix™ 88

DNA 42

Drucker, Peter, quotes 33, 51

Drucker Phenomenon, The 11

E

Edison, Thomas A., quote 125

Einstein, Albert, quote 94

Ellison, Larry (founder of Oracle) 62

Emerson, Ralph Waldo, quote 83

employee engagement
    employee behaviors 154
    example of Alpha's US Division 153-4
    example of Wicket Worldwide 150

Empowered Employee (illustration) 152

end users, definition 174

Epictetus, quote 7

executive, definition 38

executive leadership team
    definition of 16
    how CEO can assess 4
    John D. Rockefeller quote 15
    must be aligned with CEO 131
    need for tutorials 27
    not placing blame/being defensive 25
    role in strategic adjustments 45
    Russel Honoré quote 15
    team building 21
    your most expensive asset 4

Expansion Matrix™, The (illustration) 88

expectancy management 1-2

Experience Curve
    10-25% productivity improvement 11
    definition 10
    drives costs down 93
    example of not enough focus by SWT Services 78
    example of reaching critical mass by supporting Groot 71
    obstacle to delegation 137
    role in reaching critical mass 89
    underpinning product/market strategy 84

exploitation 11, 78

exploration
    can require years 11
    example of company with poor diversification program 89

example of Lewis and Clark expedition 78
role with exploitation in strategy 96

F

facilitation, professional 50

flocculation, example of concentrations 74

flow time, defined 163

focus
    example of Goliath-sized IBM vs. David-sized company 83
    focus quotients defined 163
    quote *If you chase two rabbits, both will escape* 4

forced rankings, impact on teamwork 102

Fortune 500
    divisions often operate as small businesses 5
    have over 50 times the resources 3

foul flag, following the meeting rules 28

Franklin, Benjamin
    13 point system for virtuous life 164
    quote 53

fresh frogs 19

Frog, The (meeting archetype) 19

G

Gladwell, Malcolm, author of *Outliers* 60, 137

group think 40

growth
    advocate on team 30
    bad growth 60
    Benjamin Franklin quote 53
    controlling 169
    example of Oracle doubling 13 years in a row 62
    good growth 58
    limited by team 62
    Ray Kroc quote 53
    strategic balance 43
    strategic role of 54, 64
    the ugly truths 56

H

hiring well 104-5

Holtz, Lou, quote 99

Honoré, Russel, quote 15

Hopper, Grace Murray, quote 67

Huxley, Aldous, quote 113

I

implementation

Alec Mackenzie quote   133
dictionary definition   127
empowered employees   151
four enablers of   127
four-step process   131
lean manufacturing process   116
negatives of hands-on culture   161
Peter Drucker quote   51
role of consensus   131
single point of accountability   46
team ownership   18
Thomas A. Edison quote   125
why 4-6 strategic goals   45

Innovator's Dilemma, The   61

intimacy, role in team building   28

J

Jefferson, Thomas, quote   133
Jones, John Paul, quote   67
Joyce, James, quote   1

K

Kiyosaki, Robert, quote   117
Kroc, Ray, quote   53

L

lame ducks in strategic planning   21
Law of Concentrations, The   11
Law of Critical Mass, The   12
Lombardi, Vince, quote   125
low cost provider   12

M

Mackenzie, Alec, quote from author of *The Time Trap*   133
making a living or building a business   73
Mancuso, Joseph   26
market, definition   174
measures, chose wisely   120
Michelangelo, quote   167
Mildred, managing lead-level performers   121
mission, definition   174

N

Naisbitt, John, quote   43
Newton, Isaac, quote   177

O

organization
    bond employee and position   100
    create capacity with delegation   136
    define jobs based on levels of authority   106

hire based on aptitude, attitude, and chemistry   104

match passion, competence, and alignment   102

Outliers   60

P

P/E Ratio   55, 64

Pareto Principle (80/20 Rule)   12, 101, 140, 160

participants' role in strategic planning meeting   32

participatory management, definition   24

partnership relationships   95

peer advisor groups   25, 70, 79, 170

planning

make strategic adjustments annually   45, 67, 167

process as important as the plan   30, 36-9, 50

process rather than event   46

strategic plan's six elements   36

three-step process   37

platinum paradigm, example of pilot losing alignment and passion   99

Platinum Paradigm™, The (Illustration)   101

poem about responsibility, *Everybody, Somebody, Anybody, and Nobody*   132

Politician, The (meeting archetype)   19

pricing   93

product, definition   175

product life cycle

Best company example for new market   12, 14, 76, 97

definition   12

illustrations   77

product/market strategies   85

profit

philosophical definition   93

strategic definition   93

Progress Accelerator™, The (illustration)   117

Progress Pyramid™, The (illustration)   36

Provocateur, The (meeting archetype)   20

Q

quality

(AMG's high cost)   114

cost of quality metric

INDEX

R

rationalizing legacy products, people, customers   57, 62

respect, when people's input is solicited, understood, and considered before decisions made   162

risk

   concentration

      example of Acme Manufacturing   67-8, 71-2

      example of Friend Finance   73

   managing, example of Central Pacific Railroad Company   69

   replacement technology, example of Best Systems   75

   short-term vs. long-term   72

   six major types of risk   70

Risk/Return Tradeoff, definition   62

riskiest approach to expansion   88

ropes courses   21

rules for productive meetings   32

S

Saint-Exupery, Antoine de, quote   149

sale, definition   175

Sectarian, The (meeting archetype)   20

Seneca, Lucius Annaeus, quote   21

Shaw, George Bernard, quote   23

strategic delegation   134

strategic elements, random   136

strategic laws

   The Drucker Phenomenon   11

   The Experience Curve   11

   The Law of Concentrations   11

   The Law of Critical Mass   12

   The Pareto Principle (80/20 Rule)   12

   The Product Life Cycle   12

   Risk/Reward Tradeoff   12

strategic processes

   Is it real? Can we do it? Can we win? Is it worth it?   12

   swarming   13

   What? Why? and How?   13

   Where are we now? Where do we want to be in the future? How do we change the status quo to get there?   13

swarming

   definition   13

   example of use in company turnaround   118

T

team planning
  interactive discussions   40
  process   37
  why a team?   30

Theorist, The (meeting archetype)   21

Time Trap, The   13

trust
  definition of character, competence, and caring   28
  how lack of timely responses impacts trust   162
  necessary for commitment   131
  required before granting authority   108
  role as organization's lubricant   166
  role of in sales   74

turnover, zero isn't healthy   109

V

vision, definition   175

Vistage   25, 79

visualization of strategy
  chemical reactions   9
  picture on jigsaw puzzle box   42

W

walk the talk
  company's CEO   128
  concept   155
  what employees expect   154
  why employees need coaching   154

warranty period for new employees (90 days)   104, 109

WASTE, Wait, Ask, Suggest, Tell, Empowered   106

Wooden, John - quote   113

wordsmithing, focus on content first   42

Z

Zoom   51

www.ingramcontent.com/pod-product-compliance
Lightning Source LLC
Chambersburg PA
CBHW060514090426
42735CB00011B/2218